Translated Texts for Historians

This series is designed to meet the needs of students of ancient and medieval history and others who wish to broaden their study by reading source material, but whose knowledge of Latin or Greek is not sufficient to allow them to do so in the original language. Many important Late Imperial and Dark Age texts are currently unavailable in translation and it is hoped that TTH will help to fill this gap and to complement the secondary literature in English which already exists. The series relates principally to the period 300-800 AD and includes Late Imperial, Greek, Byzantine and Syriac texts as well as source books illustrating a particular period or theme. Each volume is a self-contained scholarly translation with an introductory essay on the text and its author and notes on the text indicating major problems of interpretation, including textual difficulties.

D1559475

Front cover drawing: Bishops debating, from a medieval ivory (drawn by Gail Heather)

A full list of published titles in the Translated Texts for Historians series is printed at the end of this book.

Translated Texts for Historians
Volume 25

Hilary of Poitiers
Conflicts of Conscience and Law in the Fourth-century Church

Against Valens and Ursacius:
the extant fragments, together with his
Letter to the Emperor Constantius

Translated into English with Introduction and notes,
from the edition by Alfred Feder in *Corpus Scriptorum Ecclesiasticorum Latinorum* vol. LXV (1916) pp. 41-205,

by LIONEL R. WICKHAM

Liverpool
University
Press

First published 1997
Liverpool University Press
Senate House, Abercromby Square
Liverpool, L69 3BX

British Library Cataloguing-in-Publication Data
A British Library CIP Record is available
ISBN 0-85323-572-4

Printed in the European Union by
Bell & Bain Limited, Glasgow

CONTENTS

Acknowledgements vii

Introduction
(i) The general scope and significance of the texts ix
(ii) (a) The author xii
    (b) The background to the present texts xv
(iii) The literary history of the texts xxii

A synopsis of the fragments of
Against Valens and Ursacius
  Book One 1
  Book Two 7
  Book Three 12

A summary of Hilary's *Letter to the Emperor Constantius* 14

The texts in translation with notes.
Against Valens and Ursacius:
  Book One 15
  Book Two 70
  Book Three 93
Letter to the Emperor Constantius 104

IV. *Select Bibliography.* 110

V. *Indices* 112

ACKNOWLEDGEMENTS

I thank the managers of the Bethune-Baker Fund for a grant towards the preparation of the manuscript, and Dr Mark Elliott for putting it on disk.

Lionel R. Wickham

Introduction

(i) The general scope and significance of the texts; their translation and presentation here.

I present here in an English translation with explanatory notes, two distinct but related texts by Hilary (born probably about 320, died 367/368) earliest recorded bishop of Poitiers, distinguished Latin father, and doctor of the Western Church: *Against Valens and Ursacius* (CPL 436) and *Letter to the Emperor Constantius* (CPL 460). I start with the second, which is easier to describe. It is an open letter by Hilary addressed to the Emperor in November or December 359 and asking for an opportunity to speak to him publicly and to the bishops on hand for a council of the Church in Constantinople. Why Hilary was there and what the council's business was I shall explain below. The importance of the text is partly biographical, for it speaks (enigmatically, it must be admitted) about Hilary himself. It has another interest too, for it is an attempt to persuade an emperor, whose presumed desire to ensure to the Church a simple Biblical faith is welcomed, to take a step he had no intention whatever of taking: to throw his weight behind the proclamation of the Nicene Creed as the authoritative declaration of the Church's faith. The letter, of course, had no effect so far as we know. Hilary was not given his forum. When Constantius died, Hilary was free to express himself very differently indeed and to reveal either his attitude all along or the change of feeling wrought by disappointment. The result was the diatribe, *Against Constantius* (CPL 461)

The first text is all that remains apparently of a work written in three stages over a period of eleven years. We do not know for certain what Hilary called it, or even if he gave the whole a single title. But it went eventually under the name of *Against Valens and Ursacius,* two bishops of Mursa (Osijek) and Singidunum (Belgrade) respectively whose association with Constantius, and whose conduct and theology, Hilary thought disastrous. They figure prominently in our text, and, no doubt, would have figured even more prominently had the work survived complete. The literary history of the text I set out below. It will suffice to say here that it is almost as complex as the sequence of events which is its theme. The theme was the controversy over the doctrine of God

which divided Christians in the fourth century, connected, as that
controversy was with issues about the relations between Church and
State and about the behaviour of particular Church leaders. Hilary's
book was, of course, a product of that controversy. He himself and his
writings were ingredients in it. This book was a propagandist piece, a
work of interpretation selective in its use of evidence. Much of it must
have consisted of quotations strung together with intervening
commentary, exhortation and cries of despair. It is, for the most part,
these quotations which have been preserved (often uniquely) here, to
instruct and tease historians of the Church and its teachings. They open
a window upon Church life, to disclose disconcerting scenes of violence
and disorder, acts of gross irresponsibility and crude opportunism, and
one embarrassing betrayal of trust: the failure by Liberius, bishop of
Rome, to maintain the Church's faith. A few, depressingly few, cases
of heroism are recorded. But besides these quotations some fine lines by
Hilary have survived, an author who, whatever estimate may be given
of his command of theology in its philosophical aspects, had a gift for
the rhetorically effective and exercised it in Latin prose which the
interpreter must read aloud first to understand and then to admire. How,
then, did Hilary present the events in some of which he played a part?
As a drama, in which the consequences, of two culpable errors persisted
in, played themselves out over the Church of the Empire in East and
West. The first error was made by the Eastern Church about Athanasius,
his actions and his theology, when it libelled him as a man convicted of
violence who befriended known heretics; the second occurred when the
terms of the Nicene Creed, understood as affirming only what had
always been affirmed by Catholics, were impugned. Rectify these
mistakes, Hilary urges, and disharmony vanishes. The end of the whole
book seems to show how far the process of rectification has gone and
how much more remains in the West to be achieved.

I explain briefly the method of presentation in this volume. First, I
have made my translation from the edition of Feder. The englished title
page of what I have called *Against Valens and Ursacius* is as follows:
'EXCERPTS FROM SAINT HILARY'S LOST HISTORICAL WORK,
**SEEMINGLY IN THREE BOOKS, AGAINST VALENS AND
URSACIUS.** *A.* COLLECTED ANTIARIAN PARISIAN PIECES
(HISTORICAL FRAGMENTS). *B.* APPENDIX TO THE ANTIARIAN
PIECES: ADDRESS OF THE SYNOD OF SARDICA TO THE

EMPEROR CONSTANTIUS AND SAINT HILARY'S NARRATIVE
TEXT (BOOK ONE TO CONSTANTIUS). *C.* THREE BOOKS
AGAINST VALENS AND URSACIUS from the Collected pieces and
Appendix, book one to Constantius, as conjecturally arranged'. What I
present here does not correspond with this title page. I have set out the
fragments in the order reliably discerned by Feder (= *C.* in the title set
out above) given on pp. 191-193 of his edition. It is not the order of his
printed text. For reasons explained below he set out *A* under the heading
of two series: A and B, with numbered terms falling in them. This
numbering of *A,* and the title he used of *B* are commonly used by all
who refer to this work of Hilary's. They make no sense when the
fragments are set out in their probably correct order. The fragments
come singly or fall into groups. So I have given a number in Roman
numerals answering either to an item or a group as the case may be.
The numbers will be found in the translation beside the item or group
at its beginning. I have used them in the Synopsis and the annotations.
The Synopsis records Feder's listing and his page numbers for the items.
Those page numbers will also be found in my translation. A reverse
index is set out the end of this volume. Secondly, so far as the Latin
text is concerned, I have habitually followed what Feder printed.
Important departures I have signalled in the notes. Trivial departures,
usually when I have followed an emendation by a previous editor, noted
by Feder in his apparatus, I have left unremarked. The text is often
corrupt and does not always run smoothly even after editorial surgery.
Though I suspect a number of faults remain, I am unable to offer
anything better and venture no improvements of my own. Thirdly, I
have usually preserved in the translation the latinized Greek names e.g.
Fotinus. The index of personal names will assist in cases of doubt. I
have intended to follow Hilary's versions of those passages where the
Greek original survives. Clearly he, or whoever was responsible for the
versions, made them *currente calamo.* Though never mendacious, they
are often slightly adrift. The Greek originals ought always to be
consulted by students wishing to quote the passages for which they are
extant. Finally, as for the annotations they are limited to the minimum
I thought necessary to follow the text of a remarkable work, almost each
line of whose fascinating pages could carry a learned note. Many names
of men important in their own day weave in and out or come up for
transient mention. I have asterisked in the appropriate index those who

have rated an entry in the *Encylopedia of the Early Church* and I invite puzzled readers to turn there for some of the information that it would be superfluous to repeat here in footnotes.

(ii) (a) The author.

Hilary's life-story emerges only in disjointed episodes. We do not even know his full name, and next to nothing about his personal circumstances. The way he expresses himself tells us that he was a man of education familiar with the patterns and techniques of public speaking and debate: he had learned a great deal from the standard writer on the subject, Quintilian. These skills were not acquired, any more than a modern professional singer's can be acquired, without an extended course of training. That suggests at least that there was some money in the family to pay for it. We do not know if he had a secular career (in the appropriately modified sense in which such a phrase can be used of men of his time) but one might guess it was so. There is a wholly plausible tradition that he got married, and had a daughter called Abra: a spurious letter to her, odiously pious in tone, is printed in the same volume of CSEL that contains the present works. He tells us a little, perhaps, about a personal search for God at the beginning of his book on the doctrine of God in Trinity, but the language is stylised, conventional, giving nothing away. When he wrote the first edition of his book about the recent councils (*De Synodis* [CPL 434]) in 359, to educate the Gallican bishops on fresh developments in the interpretation of Christian doctrine, he let slip the unsurprising information (in chapter 91) that he was baptized as an adult. That tells us nothing, except that like any other normal baptizand he was given instruction (probably rather elementary instruction, though that would depend on where you were) on the story of the divine plan foreshadowed in the Old Testament and completed in Christ, and what it meant for Christian conduct. As to direct theological preparation for ministry, we have some meagre clues in what is, apparently, his first published work, a commentary on Matthew's gospel. He had mastered the standard repertoire of authorities for a Latin theologian (Novatian, Cyprian and Tertullian); if he knew any Greek writers on theology, it does not show. Bishops and prospective bishops often publish (again that is a term in need of nuancing: it means, at this time, having a work copied and sent to interested people for reading and passing on) to show that they are electable because they have something of intellectual importance to say. And the apparently scanty Church at Poitiers (Pictavium) was fortunate to secure so gifted a candidate. We do not know precisely when that happened or who ordained him. What we do know is that his career took a striking new turn, and his importance for his contemporaries and for us was dramatically enhanced, by banishment to Phrygia, in 356, after, and somehow because of, a council at Béziers (Biterrae).

Hilary speaks several times about his banishment (most importantly in the second and third paragraphs of the *Letter to Constantius*) but never says precisely why it happened. The matter has been much debated and I direct the reader to the most recent contribution to that debate, by Pieter Smulders in his fine commentary on the Preface to Hilary's work against Valens and Ursacius, for a résumé of the evidence and his proposed answer to the question. What Hilary tells us is that he was the victim of machinations by Saturninus, bishop of Arles (Arelas), who delated him to the Emperor Constantius. Banishment then followed. The puzzle is why, if the bishops of Arles and Poitiers were in contention at Béziers over a matter of doctrine (as they probably were) and if Hilary was not condemned by the council (as he stoutly maintained he was not) did the Emperor intervene? Was there a hint by Saturninus at disaffection on the part of Hilary during the brief rebellion of Silvanus in 355? Perhaps. It is curious that another bishop, Rhodianus of Toulouse, was exiled (according to Sulpicius Severus' Chronicle II, 39,7) at the same time as Hilary. Had Hilary broken communion with Saturninus (with Valens and Ursacius too) on doctrinal grounds, before any synodical determination of just cause? That was an offence against the law in 355. Compelled to appear at the synod at Béziers (as he said he was, in *Against Constantius* 2) did he there create confusion enough to justify a complaint to the Emperor through his Caesar, Julian? (Julian, we are told in the *Letter to Constantius*, had to put up with a good deal of misrepresentation over the matter.) The range of possibilities can be extended, no doubt. In any case, was it not enough to induce the sovereign to intervene, that a well-regarded metropolitan should complain imprecisely but loudly about a junior bishop? Probably. The synod of Béziers did not depose Hilary, so far as we know: we hear of no replacement for Hilary.

Exile to Phrygia was a mild sentence: Hilary was never in detention; he says he continued his ministry through his presbyters. Banished, he proceeded to become an expert in the current controversy over the doctrine of Christ's Godhead. He came to a view about the history of the controversy, about the nature of the disagreements and about the technical terms, or slogans, in vogue: he had 'never heard the Nicene creed until about to be exiled' (as he says in *On the Synods* 91). He wrote the first two books of the work against Valens and Ursacius, his *Letter to Constantius* and possibly his big book, known under the title *On the Trinity* [*De Trinitate* CPL 433]. He was present at the council of Seleucia in 359 (*On the Synods* 91) and in Constantinople for the conclusion of that assembly. He was close to the history that was being made there and which he reported. And, of course, the attempt to address the Emperor (it is the subject of the *Letter to Constantius*) failed, as we have seen, and was followed by abuse of him.

As part of the apostate Emperor Julian's plan to discomfort the bishops by leaving them to stew in their own juice (if it was truly a plan, and not the welcome by-product of a policy of deliberate disengagement) Hilary, amongst many others, returned to his see unhindered, some time in 360. He was now free to influence in person the bishops in Gaul, with whom he had kept in touch by letter. A synod in Paris, in 360/361, recognizes his expert authority in doctrine (its letter to the Eastern bishops - Book Three no. I - shows as much) and clearly in Gaul he was a powerful force, working along with Eusebius of Vercelli (who figures prominently in our texts) for a new doctrinal settlement. With other bishops of the West his relations were less fortunate. For Lucifer of Cagliari (he figures also in the work against Valens and Ursacius) Hilary was tarred with the Arian brush. Nothing would do for Lucifer except his interpretation of Nicene orthodoxy, and he excommunicated Hilary. And, in an opposite case, Hilary's attempt to unseat Auxentius, bishop of Milan (again, mentioned here) in 364 on doctrinal grounds failed. He wrote up the story in a book against Auxentius [*Against Auxentius* CPL 462]. The bishop was too much valued, Hilary's argument too flimsy, to bring down a bishop unorthodox by standards not yet universally recognized. Hilary wrote some other works about this time, of Biblical exposition [CPL 427f]; none survives complete. They belong to the most difficult genre of the ancient theology to appreciate and I do not know how much of value for the history of exegesis they contain.

The fairly brief, but busy and productive career of about 15 years, ended with his death at Poitiers in 367/368.

(b) The background to the present texts.

I shall only point here to the minimum necessary to make sense of these texts for the historians with some elementary knowledge who may wish to read them. All standard histories of early Christian life and thought deal with the period and the issues. In addition there is a large body of literature dealing with aspects of it. It is to these standard histories and mongraphs that I refer readers for more detailed accounts than I can offer here. The Synopsis and the notes to the translation will, I hope, provide further guidance to a first acquaintance with the two works. Something simple, in the way of background scheme, is required at the start.

These texts belong to a disturbed period of the Church's history: disturbed, because it was a phase of experiment in accommodation to new conditions of being. The basis of its polity had altered. It altered through the advent of the Christian Emperor Constantine and the continuation by his immediate successors of his work of promoting the Church. For it is one thing to be in essence a group, small or large, of protesters, living on sufferance which might be withheld. It had been that during the years before Constantine. It is another to be a Church which possesses power: assets (property, money, manpower) and authority (decisive influence on the promulgation of public law, access to means of coercion through the agents of law); power and the responsibility that accompanies it. It owed responsibility of course to its founder and his heavenly Father whose Spirit gave it life, so it had always been taught. It now owed it also to the Christian Emperor who expected it to provide cohesion, prosperity, moral values, revealed truth, a divine basis. In return he would guarantee its security and a framework of law and action to promote that security. So much was the general understanding. (It emerges often in our texts; strikingly in what I find the most interesting extract in them all: Constantius' letter to the Italian bishops, no. XI in Book Two of the work against Valens and Ursacius.) To have effect it was required that the Emperor know who the Church is and what it is saying; or, to put it the other way round, that the Church can define itself and speak with a united voice. It required too that the Church should continue to look after the business which properly concerned itself (its membership, the appointment of its clergy, its teaching).

I have spoken of 'the Church'. But the Church at this period was more like a confederation than a unified state. It consisted of autonomous Churches of the capital city of a province, patron (one might call it) of the other churches of the towns within it. In the cases of the apostolic sees of Rome, Alexandria and Antioch the Churches were much larger than their civil, provincial boundaries. Assemblies of bishops convened at their capital to decide and enforce policies. A good many such councils are referred to or presupposed in our texts: Tyre in 335, Antioch in 341 and 352, Arles in 353, Milan in 345, 347 and 355, Sirmium in 357, and others less important. Sometimes the Emperor played a part in their convening and was on hand at their deliberations. Especially that was so when the council met where the court was. Their decisions might be communicated elsewhere (in all these cases they were), and the general principle obtained that Churches should arrive at a common mind representing the mind of the Church as a whole. There was no sovereign Church to dictate the contents of the common mind: the 'papacy', however desirable it might be, did not yet exist. A special aura certainly surrounded the Church of Rome. Without Rome there could be no common mind. But what Rome thought was not the rule for the rest. If a common mind for all the churches of the Empire had to be found, it needed a general assembly. Constantine invented the ecumenical council to answer the need. Representatives from all the Churches would meet, agree and declare the unanimous consensus. The idea is excellent. There is an in-built dilemma, though. The Emperor must act to bring about an ecumenical council. Such councils did not and could not happen without his blessing and support. Quite apart from anything else the logistics required as much: how could, a hundred bishops be conveyed across half Asia Minor, say, without the help of the public post? The Emperor wants a notification of the consensus. The assumption is that it exists, because the Church is a divine society inspired by the Holy Ghost, but needs to be disclosed. That is sometimes the case. More often, though, it is not. And when it does not, the very fact that he has called a Council constitutes something of an intervention in the internal workings of the Churches. Moreover, if he tries by force to bring about consensus amongst often exceedingly quarrelsome people, and if having enforced consensus he backs it with the coercive powers of the state, matters will be made worse than they were before. The bishops will perhaps fail to hold an orderly assembly or they will return home and take no notice of what was allegedly decided: the council will not be 'received'. This was the special dilemma which faced the Emperor Constantius who is the most important element in the turbulent experiment in Church existence which makes up the 'Arian' controversy, a controversy with which Arius himself had little to do even though he started it off.

Three important ecumenical councils took place in the period covered by our texts: at Nicea (325), Sardica (342 or 343) and Rimini/Seleucia (359). Only the first of these represented the mind of the Church sufficiently to be numbered in the Church's lists as a received Ecumenical Council, the first of the seven of the early Byzantine period. Its creed is, for our texts, the most important thing about it. Hilary gives his Latin translation of it in Book One no. IX of his work against Valens and Ursacius. But the Council had to deal as well with a serious schism, the Melitian, affecting the Church of Alexandria. It dated back twenty years and had its origin in the 'great persecution' under Diocletian. The issue was the treatment of those who had cooperated with the secular power and had lapsed; it had nothing to do with the doctrine of God. A substantial body of clergy and people was in secession from the authority of the bishop of Alexandria under the leadership of Melitius, bishop of Assiut (Lycopolis). The Council supported the current bishop of Alexandria, Alexander, in his efforts to procure unity, and a solution to the problem of reunification, by reincorporation of Melitius' clergy within the Church catholic, was provided. Recusant Melitians still remained in large numbers and were to do so in diminishing quantity for many years (we hear of them as late as the sixth century). They were to prove almost the undoing of Alexander's successor, Athanasius (elected 328, on Alexander's death).

Besides the problem of the Melitians, there was the issue of the doctrine of God. It had been raised in an acute manner, about 318, by a presbyter of Alexandria, Arius. For Arius, though Jesus Christ was certainly 'God' both before and after his incarnation, he is as certainly distinct from his Father : consequently, he is not 'God' in the absolute sense in which his Father is God. He contradicted the teaching of Alexander publicly, gained adherents and was accordingly excommunicated. He appealed for help to leading churchmen outside Alexandria. A council was convened at Antioch in 324 which upheld his bishop, but there were dissentient voices: the most distinguished theologian of the period, Eusebius of Caesarea in Palestine, was provisionally excommunicated, and matters were left to be resolved at the forthcoming great Ecumenical Council of Nicea. It produced its creed, not the one commonly called 'Nicene' which belongs to the Council of Constantinople (381), but like it in containing the word 'homoüsios', usually translated 'consubstantial'. The word was a novelty, its meaning not explained at the time and variously interpreted. At least one reason for putting into a confession of faith this frigid term was to contradict Arius, who had repudiated it. Eusebius had difficulty with it, but was persuaded by Constantine that it was harmless and meant 'entirely like'. Disagreement about the word was to become intense, as many passages in our texts make plain. For now it was enough that Arius had been scouted. The Church had expressed its mind. The Emperor, who intervened actively in the discussions, now knew who the Church was whose cause he intended to promote.

I need say little of the Councils of Sardica and Rimini/Seleucia, what their business was and their consequences. These matters stand in the foreground of our texts. Something must be said about why they were convened, and for that we must attend to Athanasius. He had been bequeathed the problems that had faced Alexander. Though much else is disputed about him, nobody denies that he was early and fundamentally opposed to Arius' conclusions; that he proceeded vigorously against the Melitians; and that he had forces at his command able to quell opposition. His vigour produced scandal: the cases of Ischyras and Arsenius. The charges and Athanasius' rebuttal of them are given in Hilary's work against Valens and Ursacius Book One nos. IIff. Appeals were made by Athanasius' alleged victims, disciplinary church hearings appointed at Caesarea in Palestine in 334 and Tyre in 335. The accused declined to attend the first, and at the latter he was formally convicted on the reports of an investigation at the Mareotis where Ischyras claimed to have been assaulted. He took himself off 'in an open boat' to Constantinople, confronted the astonished Constantine and asked for an impartial hearing from his peers. It went against him. The

Emperor, convinced that Athanasius was a danger to public order, banished him to Trier. Constantine, though, died in 337, to be succeeded by his three sons (Constantine II, Constans and Constantius, who shared out the Empire between them) and Athanasius returned home. However, the judgement against him still stood, and he was forced out in 339. He went to Rome to make his case heard there. He was joined next year by Marcellus who had been deposed from his see, Ancyra, on doctrinal grounds. Marcellus occupies some space in Hilary's account of events, where his alleged errors are listed (Book One no. II, para. 2), his defence offered (no. III, para. 6) and Athanasius' later disavowal of tendencies implicit in his writings explained. Julius, bishop of Rome, took the unusual step (we cannot call it unconstitutional, since there was as yet no constitution governing the matter) of acting, with his synod, as a higher court of appeal. He wrote to Antioch, to the leading Eastern opponents of Athanasius who were assembling for the dedication of a splendid new church there on Epiphany 341, inviting them to a synod at Rome. The invitation was trenchantly refused, with a demand that the decisions given previously should stand. Now it was a rule that those who will not plead their cause, lose it by default. Besides which the judges were persuaded that there was no case to answer. The convictions were, therefore, quashed. Both accused were acquitted by Julius and his synod: Athanasius of the charges of violent and profane conduct; Marcellus of those of heresy.

Though the Easterns were to protest loudly about the acquittal of Athanasius later on, and at the principle of Roman appellate jurisdiction, for the moment they seem to have been more concerned about Marcellus. At any rate, they thought it worthwhile next year to try to reach a common mind about him through the good offices of the Western Emperor Constans (now sole Emperor there after the death of Constantine II). Perhaps they were induced by the Eastern Emperor, Constantius, to make the move. They sent a delegation to Constans at Trier, bearing a declaration of faith (the 'Fourth Creed of Antioch') whose main point is the condemnation of Marcellus' alleged views: it contains the phrase 'whose kingdom, being unceasing, remains for infinite ages'. Whatever Constans might do, the bishop of Trier, Maximinus, would not admit the delegates. The next move in the peace process must be an ecumenical council. The two Emperors summoned it to meet at Sardica in the autumn of either 342 or 343. The prescribed agenda is mentioned in Book One no. IV para. 3. The passage should be read with care, for it is a partisan presentation. But clearly matters of doctrine, appeals from unjust dismissal and the use of force to restore order, were to be dealt with. Two separate groups, Eastern and Western, arrived, quarrelled and denounced each other. The story tells itself in Book One nos. II - IV and X. The Council of Sardica had failed: the Western bishops claimed a right of appeal to Rome, absolved Athanasius and Marcellus of the disciplinary and doctrinal charges, and labelled their opponents 'Arians'; the Eastern bishops rejected the right of the West to overturn the decisions of Eastern councils, re-iterated the charges against Athanasius and Marcellus, and repudiated 'Arianism'.

I have called them 'Eastern bishops', and so the large majority of the group were. But they included in their ranks Valens of Mursa and Ursacius of Singidunum (though he is not a signatory to their joint letter). Hilary saw them as the villains of the drama that followed the failure of the ecumenical council. Their changes of tack are highlighted, and their failure to induce bishop Germinius to surrender on the question of doctrine ends the fragments we have of Book Three of the work Hilary directed against them. They are sometimes called by modern historians 'court bishops', a category of almost as little explanatory help, I would suggest, as 'villains'; 'advisers to the Crown', or 'trusted servants' imply either too official or too intimate a role. However you think of them, they acted with, and in some sense on behalf of, Constantius, sole ruler of the Empire after the coup in 350 by Magnentius which ended the life of Constans and Constantius' decisive defeat of the usurper at Mursa in 351. Part of the experiment in Church existence, which these years see through, comes now to a critical point. Constantius seems genuinely to have believed that consensus in the Church existed and had only to be made articulate. It would seem that he was, at bottom, right. What will happen, then, if the Emperor knocks the heads of these obstinate and quarrelsome clergy together and makes them agree? Agreement, he was convinced, was stymied by use of the word 'substance', *usia,* in formal expressions of the Christian doctrine of God. If the term is discarded, if it is affirmed simply that the Son is like the Father, and if a quarantine line is drawn between Athanasius and the rest of the Church, then unity can be achieved. Something like this, you might say, was the next step in the experiment of the accommodation of the Church to new conditions which was now tried.

The result was exceedingly expensive in terms of human misery, as Hilary's pages make plain. Constantius demanded and obtained the deposition of Athanasius at councils in Arles (353) and Milan (355). Paulinus of Trier (his fate was the starting-point for Hilary's account of things) at the one, and Eusebius of Vercelli at the other (he was a distinguished bishop representing a particularly tough-minded party), refused and were banished. He moved on to exile Liberius to Thrace in 356 (Book Two, nos. III - VI) and permit his return only on repudiation of Athanasius. Coupled with this repudiation was Liberius' assent to a creed (probably that published at Sirmium in 357), disowning, attempting to disinvent you might say, the contentious word.

The 'Blasphemy of Sirmium' (as Hilary called it in *On the Synods*, 11) had been offered by bishops of the Church. It could, perhaps, express the Church's mind. For some people, after persuasion, it had. But there were those who thought it dangerous not to address the question it raised. Basil of Ancyra (he is mentioned more than once in our texts) was an influential bishop who took that view, along with a considerable number of others in the East. They were alarmed at the anomean (dissimilarian) teaching of Aëtius (who also figures briefly) that the Son is utterly different in substance from the Sole True God, mirror image, though he is, of the Father, God in action as creative will whose created product, or 'offspring', he is. This seemed to be blasphemy in the strictest sense. Since the Son is God, he must at least, so it was thought, be like his Father in substance. So when Constantius summoned an ecumenical council to convene in two halves, at Rimini and Seleucia in 359, however tired and confused the bishops might be, however willing they might be to settle for an enforced consensus, there was a significant body of opinion which demanded that a line be drawn. They did not carry the day. Hilary gives documents, with some explanatory words of his own, which set out the procedure, and outline the course of events of which he was in part a witness (Book Two, nos. XI - XX). He sympathized, as did Athanasius who wrote his work *On the synods* [CPG 2128] for their ears, with the 'like in substance' people. In the long run it was through convincing them that the Nicene creed, with its 'consubstantial', was the only safe standard of Christian faith, that the matter reached the resolution it did. To them in a sense, the future belonged; and, unknown to Hilary, hanging on to Basil of Ancyra's coatstrings was another Basil (of Caesarea in Cappadocia), far more important than his patron, who would shape the interpretation of God in Trinity in a new and enduring way. As for the ecumenical council itself, Hilary tells us, and we are informed too from elsewhere, about the debates, the internal discussions and manoevres which ended up, at Constantinople in the winter of the year, with an apparent expression of the Church's mind: 'the Son is like the Father, as the Bible puts it'. Hilary's *Letter to Constantius* is a last-ditch attempt to get a hearing for a different slogan.

The subsequent history of the controversy extends beyond our texts. A few words only must suffice here. Constantius died in 361. His successors, Julian and Jovian, left the Church alone, for different reasons: Julian because he had his own religion, Jovian because he was too busy. Valens took up again the policy of Constantius; Valentinian in the West was more attuned to the prevailing mood of the Church. For East and West were uniting round the Nicene standard and the doctrine of God it was felt to secure uniquely. The texts of Book Three, nos. I and IV hint at a process gathering momentum. When the Emperor Theodosius issued his edict to all peoples on February 27th 380 comanding obedience to the Nicene faith, he was underwriting a consensus which in general obtained.

(iii) The literary history of the texts.

[a] *Against Valens and Ursacius* : the extant fragments.

I offer here a brief account of Feder's exposition of the matter as he gives it in his Preface pp. XX - LXIX. It is a headache. I start with the first edition of the text which was produced in Paris in 1598 by Nicholas Le Fèvre (Faber). It was based on the work of Peter Pithou who used a 15th century manuscript (=T) now lost. Pithou died when the edition he was preparing was in the press, and Le Fèvre. misunderstanding the order of the texts, rearranged them. The next editor, Pierre Coustant (Coustantius) in 1693, with a fine eye for difficulties in the readings of the text but a misdirected zeal for temporal order, rearranged them again. Coustant's edition, which took note of Sirmond (see below) was reprinted in 1845, with minor additions from Scipione Maffei's Verona edition of 1730, in J. P. Migne's Patrologia Latina tome 10, the standard collection of re-prints of editions of patristic and early medieval texts still in use where no better are available. (The great Eduard Schwartz, who understood these Church controversies almost better than anyone else ever has, called it more of a sewer than a patrology.) The order of the manuscript was restored by Feder for his edition, where the fragments (they are *A.* on Feder's title page - see above) are divided into two blocks, Series A and Series B. He used a ninth century manuscript in the Bibliothèque de l'Arsenal in Paris (=A) of which manuscript T (see above) was a copy. One other manuscript (=S), of comparable importance with manuscript A is known to have existed in the library of Saint Remigius in Rheims but it is now lost. Manuscript S was used by Jacques Sirmond (Sirmondus) in his 1629 edition of the Gallic Councils (Concilia Antiqua Galliae I). The date of S is unknown, but it appears to have been independently derived from the common source of manuscripts A and S. Unfortunately Sirmond evidently mingled conjectures of his own with reports of its readings; the results for the reliability of his information will be obvious. Effectively, there is a single manuscript, A, of loosely connected fragments of Hilary's work, though items appearing in the source of manuscript A (notably the budget of letters by Liberius in Book Two, and the letter of the Western bishops at Sardica (Book One, no. IV)) were extracted for use in other collections, the readings there being taken note of by Feder. Moreover, a good number of the documents that Hilary used are extant either in the original language or in versions, elsewhere (see my notes to the translation).

A special word must be said about what is given in the present translation as Book One, nos. X, the Synod of Sardica's address to Constantius, and XI, Hilary's narrative. (It is *B.* in Feder's title page, see above). These do not form part of the series of fragments transmitted in manuscript A. Instead they appear as a single item in various manuscripts, mostly of the 12th but one of the sixth century, often under the heading: Book One to Constantius (*Liber I ad Constantium*). The designation is clearly old: because the sixth century manuscript refers to it as coming from 'book one of Saint Hilary to Constantius'; and Ferrandus, writing at roughly the same time, apparently thinks of it, in chapter 2 of a letter to Pelagius and Anatolius [CPG 848], as belonging to Hilary's *first* 'book he wrote to the Emperor Constantius'. Similarly, Sulpicius Severus, writing much nearer to

Hilary's time, in about 403, speaks in his Chronicle [= CPL 474] book
II c. 45, of three books written by Hilary in which Hilary asked for a
hearing from the Emperor i.e. probably: a *Book One*, whose contents we
shall consider below; a *Book Two*, which is the *Letter to Constantius*;
and a *Book Three*, which is the diatribe *Against Constantius*. Jerome,
writing very close to the time of Hilary, in his short notes on famous
authors (*De Viris Illustribus* c. 100) [CPL 616], does not know of three
books with Constantius in the title, however, but only of two: the
diatribe *Against Constantius* and the *Letter to Constantius* translated
here. Leaving aside the question of title, there is the question of content.
Here we have not a single piece, but two pieces: an address from a
group of people to an Emperor, followed by commentary from an
individual. It is to the credit of the Benedictine scholar André Wilmart
to have seen that we have here another portion of the work of which
fragments remain in manuscript A, and that it fits into place after the
exposition and discussion of the Nicene creed.

As has been said, Feder divided the fragments into two series, Series
A and Series B. The rationale of this is that in manuscript A, Series B
is headed in the index to the manuscript *Bishop Hilary of Poitiers' book*
(Liber sancti hilarii pictavensis episcopi) and concluded in the text *Here
ends Saint Hilary's* sc. writing/text *from the historical work*. Series A
does not have these mentions of a historical work of Hilary from which
they are extracted. They follow an excerpt from Hilary's *On the Trinity*
and so are associated with him without naming him. The likenesses
between the two series are apparent: documents linked by, or introduced
by, commentary. That they all come from a work by Hilary is as certain
as anything of this kind can be.

Not certain, but very likely, is the hypothesis that they all, together
with the so-called *Book One to Constantius*, formed part of a book by
Hilary which started as a single volume *Against Valens and Ursacius*
(written in 356) and acquired sequels in 359/360 and 367. The evidence
is as follows. (1) Jerome (loc. cit.) knows of a 'book' by Hilary 'against
Valens and Ursacius, containing a history of the synod of
Rimini/Seleucia'. So also does Rufinus (*On the falsification of Origen's
books* [CPG 198a]), though he does not mention the pair of personal
names. (2) A group of fragments starting with a preface and continuing
with texts relating to the Council of Sardica and the innocence of
Athanasius cohere. In these Hilary refers to the Council of Arles 353

and to the condemnation of Athanasius at Milan 355 (see Book One: Preface, para. 6 - the case of Paulinus; no. XI, para. 3 - the recent matter of Eusebius of Vercelli). Moreover, though here we verge upon the moot, the synod at Béziers of 356 and its hostility to Hilary appear to be referred to in the Preface para. 5 (towards the end), as the occasion for Hilary's writing: he will set out clearly what he was not able to say then. (3) Phoebadius of Agen in a work *Against the Arians* [CPL 473], to be dated 358, makes use of passages from Hilary's narrative in Book One nos. 8f. (The influence is clearly displayed in Smulders' Excursus V, see bibliography.) 4) So also does Gregory of Elvira in his *On the Faith* [CPL 551], to be dated after 360. (The careful reader will spot them in the text: they stick out by the use of keywords and phrases, or trains of argument, gratefully lifted by Gregory from Hilary. I have repeated Feder's references to them in the annotations). From (1) it is evident that Hilary wrote a book against Valens and Ursacius that was known and used; from (2) and (3) that the fragments we have belong to a book in circulation by 358. Now from (1) it follows that his book cannot be identical with the work known to Jerome and Rufinus. They link the book they know with the Council of Rimini/Seleucia. But the coherent group of fragments mentioned in (2) belong to a book prior to the council: the historical events marked as 'recent' are of the the years 353 and 355. Yet Jerome apparently knows only of a single work. If there was only a single work, then it must have contained material dealing with the Council of Rimini/Seleucia and forming a continuation of the work known to Phoebadius: a Book Two. For, (5) our manuscript, A, does contain such material which apparently belongs together. Moreover, in the narrative text, Book Two no. XX, Hilary expostulates with the errant bishops who came from Rimini to Constantinople and betrayed their trust. Hilary went from Seleucia to Constantinople and attempted to dissuade the delegates from Rimini assenting to the formula of faith approved at Nice and Rimini. That assent was given on the 31st of December 359. It is likely, then, that these passages relating to Rimini/Seleucia were part of a text written in 359/360. (6) It may well be that the excerptor of the fragments, or some later learned editor, knew of the existence of a Book Two, because of the heading in the text (but not the index) of manuscript A (see above). With these fragments relating to Rimini/Seleucia (if what has been adduced above is accepted, Book Two) plausibly cohere the group of letters from Liberius of Rome. More cannot be said: it is plausible. But assuming that those letters belong with the fragments in some way, this is a reasonable place to assign them: they will go to explain the pressures and difficulties which produced the debâcle of Constantinople. Now, we also have passages (they do not contain any narrative comment by Hilary) which do not belong with our presumed Book Two of 359/360. The last of these is dated 18th December 366 (Book Three, no. VI). They have the same form as the other fragments. Granted the testimony of Jerome to a single book and a general coherence of theme with the two Books of 356 and 359/360, we may guess that Hilary wrote a continuation between 366 and his death a year or so later. It is a guess worth making, if we concede that the fragments of our manuscript, A, are, with with what are designated in the translation as Book I, nos. Xf (see above), excerpts of an originally continuous text. Why precisely the extracts were made and when, is not certain. The presumption is that somebody in the sixth or seventh centuries copied out the highlights of Hilary's *Against Valens and Ursacius* and somebody a couple of centuries later put them all together in the way they appear in manuscript A. The excerptor was not interested in Book One, nos. Xf. That passage, though, had also been excerpted by somebody rather earlier and survived elsewhere on its own.

[b] *Letter to Constantius* (Liber II ad Constantium).

The manuscripts containing this also transmit the so-called 'Book One to Constantius' (Liber I ad Constantium = [in the translation] Book One nos. Xf) and the diatribe *Against Constantius* (Liber Contra Constantium - see above). The designation 'Second book to Constantius' is, as said above, old. Ferrandus quotes part of it (loc. cit. above), Jerome (loc. cit.) mentions a short book to Constantius, written by Hilary to the Emperor then living at Constantinople. Sulpicius Severus (loc. cit.) speaks of Hilary's request for a royal audience in order to debate the faith in the presence of his opponents, at a time when Hilary perceived extreme danger to the faith with the deception of the Westerns (sc. at Nice) and the possibility of the defeat of the Easterns. This is our text.

A synopsis of the fragments of
Against Valens and Ursacius.

Book One (written in 356)

[I]   A Preface [= Series B I pp. 98-102] in which Hilary, after an exordium on the theological virtues and a declaration of his own sincerity [1-3] sets out the theme of the book: [4-5] the complex disagreement which has led to the summoning of church councils and to disturbances in the churches. [6] Certain bishops have been exiled for refusing to condemn Athanasius and the issues at stake have been personalized, whereas they concern the substance of Catholic faith. [7] Hilary will make the religious issues plain by giving a historical account of the whole case, beginning from the recent refusal of Paulinus, bishop of Trier, to condemn Athanasius (353), which resulted in his banishment (to Phrygia) Close attention is called for from the reader, but the mattters are important. [An account of Paulinus' exile and of the Council of Arles will have followed. The subsequent fragments of this book all relate to the Councils of Serdica (342 or 343 - the date is contested) and Milan (355)].

[II] A *letter of the Eastern bishops* [= Series A IV pp. 48-78] headed by Stephen of Antioch at the Council of Serdica to certain named bishops, and sent to Africa. [1] The faith of the Church and its discipline is at stake. [2] Marcellus of Ancyra has been teaching profanity: Christ's sovereignty began with his advent and will end with the end of the world; he is not the 'image of the invisible God' in his own eternal being but in the same way that he became 'bread', 'door' and 'life' at his bodily conception. It is teaching which mixes Sabellianism (sc. Christ as a temporary manifestation of the single divine subject) with Paul of Samosata's teaching (sc. that a man, Jesus, had become the dwelling-place of the Word) and Montanus' (sc. of successive phases of revelation by Father, Son and Paraclete). [3] Marcellus' teaching had been rejected at a council in Constantinople, and he himself deposed (c.335). [4] But he has travelled abroad and falsely persuaded bishops to receive him into communion. He has acquired supporters even from those who signed his condemnation. [5]

The recipients of the letter are warned against him and his book. [6] As for Athanasius, he has committed acts of violence and desecration: profanation of the sacraments, breaking a chalice, demolishing a church; securing the imprisonment of Scyras (Ischyras); persecution of opponents. [7] He was condemned at a council in Tyre (335) by a synod of bishops from Asia Minor, but appealed to the Emperor Constantine who recognized the justice of the sentence and exiled him. [8] He returned from exile and has repeated his campaign of violence, before going into exile again. [9] Other deposed bishops and their acts of violence are named: Paul of Constantinople, Marcellus (again), Asclepas of Gaza, Lucius of Adrianopolis. [10] These have joined forces with Athanasius who has managed to persuade various bishops, including Julius of Rome, of his innocence. These having once sided rashly with Athanasius could not withdraw their support. [11] The judges who condemned Athanasius were justified in view of his association with other deposed bishops. Athanasius and Marcellus have procured a reconsideration of their cases from bishops remote from the scene of the crimes and ignorant of the facts, after the death of many of the original judges and witnesses. [12] The pair wanted to secure an acquittal from Eastern bishops, from a packed court of colluding judges. They hoped to establish a rule that Eastern bishops should be tried by Western. [13] They are now in communion with bishops they once condemned. [14] Julius, Maximin of Trier and Ossius of Cordoba favoured Athanasius and took charge of the council at Serdica ordered by the Emperor. On arrival at Serdica we found the pair received into communion by Protogenes of Serdica and Ossius. [15] We advised them to respect the previous judgements [16f.] and not to introduce a new rule about appeals; but they refused, frightened of being condemned for canonical disobedience themselves. [18] We proposed a re-examination of the question of Athanasius' sacrilege at Mareotis; it was refused. [19] Other deposed persons, guilty of various crimes arrived at Serdica and were favoured by Ossius and Protogenes. They stirred up public disorder with false propaganda. [20f.] Ossius' and Protogenes' council was a medley of ill-assorted and unprincipled people. [22] They threatened reports to the Emperor. [23] We decided to leave Serdica and report our judgement, because we will not accept Athanasius and Marcellus who have been justly condemned. [24] Do not communicate with Ossius, Protogenes, Athanasius, Marcellus, Asclepas, Paul or Julius or their associates! [25] Church and State have been set in disarray over two scoundrels, who should be shunned. [26] Their attempt to change the rules about councils is a tactic to validate their illegal acts. [27f.] The offending bishops, most prominent of whom are Julius and Ossius, are condemned and deposed. [29] A creed, with anathematisms, is set out [= Series A IV,2 pp. 67-73]. The signatures of 73 bishops follow [= Series A IV,3 pp. 74-78].

[III] An *encyclical letter* [= Series B II, 1 pp. 103-126] from the opposing side at Serdica. (Hilary's explanation, preceding it, for the inclusion of this and the following documents, will have been lost). [1] Arian heretics have done much harm to the Church. The Emperors, in consequence, have convened a council to settle the dogmatic issue. Bishops came to it from the East, likewise by imperial invitations, in connexion with false reports about Athanasius and Marcellus. [2] Complaints against the pair had been sent some time ago by a group of bishops headed by Eusebius to Julius of Rome; attestations to their innocence had also been received. Julius invited Eusebius and the rest to make good the complaints in person, but they refused. The reason is now apparent from their refusal to attend this synod: their complaint is a fabrication. [3f.] Moreover, they dared not attend because of their attested acts of violence over and above their offences against Athanasius and Marcellus. [5] We examined the alleged misdeeds of Athanasius and found the charges wholly baseless: the allegedly murdered Arsenius is alive; there is documentary testimony to the fact that Scyras (Ischyras) was sick in his cell when the profanation of the eucharist allegedly took place; evidence was received that there never had been a Melitian church in the Mareotis nor was Ischyras a Melitian presbyter. [6] The complaints against Marcellus are based on misrepresentation, and the minutes of proceedings at Antioch, where Eusebius was present, were cited as proof of his innocence. [7] Moreover, the present complainants have promoted Arians. The leaders (most of whom were signatories to the previous document) are named; these kept the rest of their Eastern companions back from participation in the synod. [8] Their crimes of violence, and above all, their Arianism, condemn them; but we find Athanasius, Marcellus and Asclepius innocent of the charges, and the intruders in their sees we depose. Do not communicate with these evil people! For the sake of unity, confirm our decision!

[IV] A *letter to Julius of Rome* [= Series B II, 2 pp. 126-130] from the previous, reporting on the synod. [1] Like Paul, Julius was present in spirit (Col. 2:5) at the synod, though absent in the flesh owing to pastoral obligations. We bishops refer to the apostolic throne the concerns of all the churches. [2] News of the proceedings has been conveyed orally and in writing. The gist is now written down. The Eastern bishops, led by Arians, refused to associate with us because we believe Athanasius and Marcellus innocent: their opponents had refused to attend a hearing in Rome; and 80 bishops testified for Athanasius. [3] Three items were on the agenda proposed by the Emperors: (i) the dogmatic question; (ii) a reconsideration of cases of alleged unjust removal from office, and therewith a right to restoration were injustice proven; (iii) the harassment of opponents of the Arian and Eusebian heresy by its ringleaders, and their malpractices. [4] Ursacius of Singidunum and Valens of Mursa have been spreading heresy and are excommunicated. Moreover, Valens is guilty of changing churches and of securing the death of bishop Viator in Aquileia. [5] Please notify our decisions elsewhere. The opponents are deposed, Athanasius and Marcellus accepted. A list of deposed [= Series B II, 3 p. 131] and of 59 signatories to the decision [= Series B II, 4 pp. 131-139] is given.

[V[*Hilary's narrative* and explanation continue [= Series B II, 5 pp. 140-143]. [1f.] The proof has been given that the accusations against Athanasius were false. [3] Honesty demands that Athanasius be acquitted, and only force could make anybody think otherwise. What of Marcellus and Fotinus? [4] Fotinus of Sirmium had been taught by Marcellus of Ancyra. Condemned at a synod in Milan (345) he was condemned two years later at a synod comprising many bishops from different provinces (Sirmium, 347) . The bishops were at pains to avoid a repetition of the disagreements at Serdica. Ursacius and Valens took the opportunity to make their peace with Julius of Rome and were received into communion after a recantation.

[VI] Letter *addressed to Julius, by Valens and Ursacius* [= Series B II, 6 pp. 143-144]. Valens and Ursacius recant (see [V]) and unreservedly withdraw all allegations against Athanasius; they undertake to take no part in any litigation without Julius' consent; the teachings of Arius are disavowed by name, and of Marcellus and Fotinus without mention of name. A note [= Series B II, 7 p. 145] by Hilary dates the letter.

[VII] Letter *by the same to Athanasius* [= Series B II, 8 p. 145]. The letter re-institutes Church communion.

[VIII] *Hilary's narrative* and explanation continue [= Series B II, 9 pp. 146-150]. [1] Valens and Ursacius were restored to communion, but Fotinus, deposed at a synod at Sirmium (347), could not be ejected. (A lacuna of uncertain extent follows). The text goes on to describe Athanasius' relations with Marcellus, who had been restored by the council of Serdica after a reading of his book (see above, no. 3 para. 6). When Marcellus went further and broached the doctrines of his pupil, Athanasius withdrew from him. The withdrawal, without condemnation either of Marcellus or his book, anticipated Fotinus' condemnation. [2] Marcellus was never condemned by a properly informed synod, but the Easterns used the condemnation of Fotinus to connect Marcellus with Athanasius and wrote so in a letter (which Hilary cited but which is not now extant). The 'Arians' unfairly condemned both Marcellus and Athanasius on the basis of Marcellus' book dealing with the subjection of Christ. The Western report of Fotinus' condemnation was simply intended for information, not to condemn Athanasius with Marcellus. [3] The severance of relations between Marcellus and Athanasius was by mutual understanding. The behaviour cannot be faulted. [4] The Easterns' letter contained a brief creed at the beginning, before passing on to condemn Fotinus and Athanasius and 'the Catholic faith'. The previous account of the synod at Serdica makes plain the falsehood of the attacks on Athanasius. Hilary will look at this creed [5] and first he remarks upon the need for creeds and [6] of the occasion [7] for the publication of the Nicene Creed.

[IX] The *Nicene* Creed [= Series B II, 10 p. 150] with commentary [= Series B II, ll pp. 151-154] now follows. [1] Its declaration of the unity of Father and Son is contrasted with the [2] other creed (see above

[VIII] para. 4), which renders the Son non-eternal and non-divine. [3f.] The Trinity of the other creed is a divided, disparate triad; [5] whereas the Nicene teaches the equal eternity and Godhead of Father and Son by the term 'homoüsion', whose meaning is explained; and its description of the incarnation sets forth the mysteries of our salvation. [6] Athanasius championed it and used it to rout Arians, who rigged accusations against him. The doctrinal basis will be understood from the following:-

[X] The *Synod of Sardica's address to Constantius* [= Liber I *Ad Constantium* 1-5, pp. 181-184]. This document from the Western bishops [1] invites the Emperor first to restrain civil functionaries from intervening in Church affairs. [2] Let liberty be given to Catholics to pursue their religion, free from Arian oppression! Let the magistrates show no partiality to heretics! [3] It is the Arians who are creating the troubles. [4] Bring back the exiled bishops! [5] It is Arian heresy which is ruining the Church.

[XI] *Hilary's narrative* continues [= Liber I *Ad Constantium* 6-8, pp. 184-187], and [1] he starts by commenting that it was appropriate for the Synod to write to the Emperor and acquaint him with their decisions. Religious truth is not to be imposed by coercion: God invites our voluntary obedience. The Arians, though, exercise compulsion and seek the support of the secular arm. [2] But the absurdity and baselessness of the Arian allegations is plain. [3] Hilary passes on to the recent matter of Eusebius of Vercelli. After the synod of Arles (353) at which Paulinus of Trier was condemned (see above [I] para. 6) Eusebius was summoned to a synod at Milan (355). Required to subscribe against Athanasius, he first asked for an examination of the orthodoxy of the judges. He would subscribe against Athanasius, if they would subscribe the Nicene Creed. Valens roughly interrupted the proceedings, popular agitation ensued and the synod had to adjourn to the palace... [At this point the fragments from the first book apparently cease.]

Book Two (written 359/360)

(No preface to the book survives. The extant fragments start apparently with a group of letters by Liberius of Rome).

[I] *Letter to the Eastern bishops* [= Series B III, 2, p. 155] (written from exile in 357). This encyclical records that Liberius had received a letter from the Easterns addressed to Julius his predecessor (died early in 352). Liberius had duly summoned Athanasius to appear in Rome, in connexion with the charges laid against him. Athanasius had refused and was in consequence condemned. The Eastern bishops are to know that Liberius is in communion with them.

[II] *Hilary continues his narrative and explanation* [= Series B III, 2 pp. 155-156]. This letter (probably the preceding) has nothing amiss in it. But Potamius (of Lisbon) and Epictetus (of Centumcellae=Civita Vecchia) were not satisfied (sc. they demanded a subscription to a doctrinal formula besides the condemnation of Athanasius). Fortunatianus of Aquileia (confidant of Liberius) circulated the letter to various bishops but was unsuccessful (sc. in securing their support for Liberius); indeed, severing communion with Athanasius proved counter-productive, since the synod of Serdica had acquitted Athanasius and letters of support for him from Egypt and Alexandria continued to circulate. The proof that Liberius had received such letters is given in the following piece.

[III] *Liberius' letter to Constantius* [= Series A VII pp. 89-93], (353/4), [1] begins by recalling the regrettable disagreement now obtaining between Liberius and Constantius. Constantius has, indeed, sent a public message indicating displeasure with Liberius who expresses a desire for true peace with the Emperor. Liberius has held the council agreed to by Constantius, and at it the issues of the man and of the faith were on the agenda. [2] The complaint has been made that the case against Athanasius was not fairly put. It is groundless: the Easterns' letters were read to the Italian bishops, but the evidence for Athanasius was stronger. The dossier on Athanasius was brought by a certain Eusebius (from Egypt). Subsequent documents have been conveyed to Arles to support the case for a council. [3] Liberius swears to his own integrity in the conduct of his office; and [4] rejects the call to peace from Eastern bishops, who include four avowed Arians and associates of Arians. [5] The Emperor has received letters from parties recently arrived. They have promised to follow the Easterns if the Easterns condemn Arius. The Easterns discussed the matter with them but answered that Arius' teaching was not in question, only the status of Athanasius. Will the Emperor, then, countenance a re-consideration of Athanasius apart from the dogmatic question? [6] The Emperor is exhorted to remember the favours of Christ towards him and to summon a council of bishops to settle matters in accordance with the Nicene exposition of faith ratified in the presence of Constantine. Liberius hopes that Constantius will look favourably upon this request.

[IV] *Letter of Liberius* (355) to the exiled Eusebius, Dionysius and Lucifer collectively [= Series B VII, 2 pp. 164-166], preceded by a note by Hilary [= Series B VII, 1 p. 164]. [1] They are martyrs for the faith. [2] Liberius asks for their prayers and news.

[V] A line from a *Letter of Liberius* to Caecilian [= Series B VII, 4 p. 166] noted by Hilary [= Series B VII, 7 p. 167) as before Liberius' exile; and a paragraph from a
[VI] *Letter of Liberius* [= Series B VII, 6 p. 167] to Ossius deal, as noted by Hilary [= Series B VII, 5 ibid], with the defection of Vincentius (of Capua). Sent as legate to the council appointed to meet in Aquileia (but actually meeting at Arles, 353), he had fallen in with the opponents' demands.

[VII] *Letter of Liberius to the Easterns* [= Series B VII, 8 pp. 168-70, (357) preceded by an explanation by Hilary [= Series B VII, 7 pp. 167-168], in which Liberius renounces Athanasius and declares his adherence to a creed set forth at Sirmium. A rebuttal of Liberius and anathematisms (by a scribe) interrupt the text. Liberius asks for his release from exile, following his agreement with the Eastern bishops.

[VIII] Hilary gives a *List of bishops* [= Series B VII, 9 p. 170] who signed a creed at Sirmium (in 351).

[IX] *Letter of Liberius* from exile (355-357) [= Series B VII, 10 pp. 170-72] to Ursacius, Valens and Germinius (of Sirmium). [1] Liberius declares his voluntary assent, for the good of peace, to the condemnation of Athanasius. He had condemned him before he informed the Emperor that Rome agreed with the Easterns in the matter. He was slow in writing to the Easterns because he wanted the simultaneous recall of the exiles. [2] He has asked Fortunatianus to convey to the Emperor his *Letter to the Eastern Bishops* (= see above [VII]). Please will they ask the Emperor for his (Liberius') restoration, and inform Epictetus and Auxentius (of Milan) of the reconciliation with them.

[X] *Letter of Liberius* from exile to Vincentius [= Series B VII,11 pp. 172-173]. [1] Liberius is in personal distress, deprived of supportive companionship. [2] Vincentius is asked to write to the bishops of Campania to tell them of Liberius' agreement with the Easterns (see above [VII]) and get them to plead with the Emperor for his (Liberius') return. An urgent request for Vincentius' help ends the letter.

[There follows a group of documents connected with the Synod of Rimini:-]

[XI] *The Emperor Constantius' Letter* [= Series A VIII pp. 93-94] to the Italian bishops at the synod of Rimini (359), dated May 28th. [1] Law derives its religious authority from the Church and it is his duty to ensure that the bishops maintain the Church's order and doctrinal concord. [2] The Italian bishops are to deal only with matters affecting them. On completion of the business, ten legates are to be sent to the court to discuss doctrinal matters with the Easterns. The council at Rimini is not to make any decisions affecting Eastern bishops; any such decision will be null and void.

[XII] *The definition of faith* accepted by Catholics at Rimini [= Series A IX, 1 pp. 95-96], maintains the unaltered profession in the tradition from Christ and the apostles, as affirmed, in opposition to heresy, at Nicea. The word 'substance' in the definition (of Nicea) is not to be repudiated (as it had been at the Council of Sirmium) as innovation.

[XIII] An *extract from the minutes of the Synod* [= Series A IX, 3 pp. 96-97], dated 21st July 359, preceded by a *Note from Hilary* [= Series A IX, 2 p. 96]. The assembled bishops reaffirm the condemnation of Ursacius, Valens, Germinius and Gaius (of Illyricum) for seeking to overthrow the decisions of Nicea and introducing a heretical creed of their own.

[XIV]   *Report of the Synod at Rimini to the Emperor* [= Series A V, 1pp. 78-85]
[1] The Western bishops have met, as ordered, at Rimini, to clarify the faith. They agreed that the traditional faith had been stated correctly and precisely at Nicea in the presence of the Emperor's father, and that it is not to be tampered with. [2] It is a barrier to Arianism and when Ursacius and Valens were accused of it before, they obtained pardon from the council of Milan (see above Book One, [IV] para. 4 and [V] para. 4). The creed of Nicea was carefully composed and since there has been a revival of heresy it is wisest to stick to it; they rejected the new creeds produced by Ursacius, Valens, Germinius and Gaius. The legates they are sending have been instructed to preserve the creed and assure the Emperor that Ursacius and the rest cannot procure peace by repudiating it. [3] Please prevent innovation; and please order the council to end and the bishops to go home. The legates will notify the Emperor of the subscribing bishops and another document conveys the names too.

[XV] *Hilary's narrative* [= Series A V, 2 p. 85] explains that ten legates from the opposing sides at Rimini were sent to the Emperor, who received only the heretical party. The Catholic legates caved in. The story is told in:-

[XVI] An *extract from the minutes of a meeting at Nice* (in Thrace) [=Series A V, 3 pp. 83-86] dated 10th October 359. [1] 14 bishops are named. Rest(it)utus, of Carthage, declares that the assembly at Rimini produced acrimony and discord, resulting in the excommunication of Ursacius and the rest. [2] Further discussion (he says) has now revealed that they are truly Catholic and are not, and have never been, heretics. The bishops agree to nullify the proceedings at Rimini and restore communion.

[XVII] *Hilary* [= Series A V, 4 p. 86] sets down the creed, brought by Valens to Rimini (see above [XIV]) and subscribed at Nice. (A passage containing the formula is probably lost).

[XVIII] A *Letter to the Emperor Constantius* from the Western bishops at Rimini [= Series A VI pp. 87-881 opposed to the writers of [XIV]: four are named. [1] We have gladly complied with the Emperor's command to disown 'usia' and 'homoüsios' in professions of faith. We report the defeat of those who opposed this wise decision. [2] We are in agreement with the Easterns (sc. at Seleucia). Please may we go home. [3] We have informed the Easterns of our agreement with them.

(Some narrative and explanation by Hilary will have preceded:-)
[XIX] *Letter from the Eastern bishops* (sc. at Seleucia) [= Series B VIII, 1 pp. 174-175] given to the delegates from the Western council at Rimini. The letter is addressed from 18 named bishops to nine named bishops, headed by Ursacius and Valens, and other unnamed delegates of the synod of Rimini. [1] Announcing themselves as of the 100-strong synod, and as having so far refrained from ecclesiastical association, they warn of the Anomean heresy, spread by Aëtius. The Emperor, too, has been apprised of it and has expressed his disapproval. There is a risk that Aëtius personally, and not the doctrines, will be condemned. The Western churches are being informed of developments.

[XX] *Hilary's narrative* [= Series B VIII, 2 pp. 175-177] and explanation of the previous texts continues. [1] He criticizes the Western delegates of the previous text. They went from Seleucia to Constantinople and sided with the heretics, failing to heed the warning by the disaffected Easterns named above. [2] They publicly interpreted Rimini's 'not a creature like one of the creatures' in the sense that the Son *is* a creature but uniquely so, and 'he is not from non-existents but from God' in the sense that his origin is God's will. Other hypocritical interpretations are detected too. [3] They have failed to observe even the faith they adhered to at Nice; and support for blasphemy has come from some book (by Valens and Ursacius?) . The changes of mind indicate enmity towards Christianity.

(The fragments from Book Two apparently end here)

Book Three (written 367)

(No preface, if there was one to the book, survives.)

[I] *Letter about the Creed from a synod of Gallican bishops at Paris to the Eastern bishops* (c.360 or 361) [= Series A I pp. .43-46]. [1] A letter entrusted to Hilary by Eastern bishops tells of the doctrinal disagreements. The majority at Rimini and Nice were forced to disown the use of 'usia'. [2] They themselves accept the 'homoüsion' and interpret it to imply the Son's full Godhead. [3] They repudiate 'he did not exist before he was born', as implying temporal origin for the Son. He is inferior to the Father as incarnate. [4] They have learned from Hilary that the legates who went from Rimini to Constantinople would not condemn the blasphemous omission of 'usia'; they repudiate this sin of ignorance, and have excommunicated Auxentius (of Milan), Ursacius, Valens, Gaius, Megasius and Justin (sees of last three unknown) in accordance with the Eastern request and in agreement with Hilary. Wrongful depositions and appointments, and refusal of 'homoüsion' with its proper implications, are condemned. Saturninus (of Arles) was condemned before and is excommunicated by all the Gallican bishops.

[II] *Letter from Eusebius bishop of Vercelli to Gregory bishop of Elvira* [= Series A II pp. 46-47 (c.360). [1] Eusebius has had a letter from Gregory telling of his opposition to Ossius, his adherence to the Nicene creed, and his repudiation of the majority at Rimini who sided with Valens and Ursacius. Continue the struggle by the pen! [2] This is my third exile. The Arians only succeed through secular protection. Write to us of your progress!

[III]   *Letter from Liberius to the Italian bishops* (362/363) [= Series B IV, 1 pp. 156-157]. [1] We are to be gentle with the penitent. The rank and file signatories at Rimini were in ignorance and moreover leniency is being shown in Egypt and Greece. [2] Penitents are to affirm the Nicene faith and repudiate the ring-leaders, recusants to be excommunicated.

[IV] *Letter of the Italian bishops to the bishops of Illyricum* [= Series B IV, 2 pp. 158-159] (363). The Italians' unity in upholding the Nicene creed and in rejecting the formula of Rimini, and their pleasure in the similar progress in Illyricum, are announced. The Illyrican bishops are invited to subscribe the creed, which excludes Arianism and Sabellianism and, by implication, Fotinus' teaching, and to rescind the decisions of Rimini. The condemnation of Arianism is not a new measure, but of long standing.

[V] Extract from a letter (366) containing *A profession of faith by Germinius* (bishop of Sirmium) [= Series A III pp. 47-48], in opposition, according to the heading, to the Arian profession. It speaks of 'likeness in all things' between Father and Son.

[VI] *A Letter* dated 18th December 366 *from Valens, Ursacius and the Illyrian bishops Gaius and Paul at Singidunum to Germinius* [= Series B V pp. 159-60].
[1] Germinius has met Valens and Paul and been advised to clarify his position. He refused but answered by letter that he remained in communion with the present writers. The writers now ask for his re-affirmation of assent to the creed of Rimini with its simple assertion of 'likeness' between Father and Son. Anything different will restore Basil (of Ancyra's) formula (of 'likeness of substance') which led to the Council of Rimini at which it was rejected. [2] Germinius is asked to make it plain that 'like in all things'. except ingeneracy, is not his profession.

[VII] *Germinius' response to certain named Illyrian bishops* (366) [=Series B VI pp. 160-164]. [1] The writer has learned that the recipients want to know the objections of Valens and his party to Germinius' creed. Germinius' creed is the same as the recipients' : faith is in Christ, the Son of God, like the Father in all things save ingeneracy. The Son's generation is unknown except by the Father. The Bible is quoted to indicate the function and status of the Son in creation and redemption, and his complete likeness to the Father. [2] The scriptural predicates 'made' and 'created' refer, as do 'door', 'way' etc., to the conditions of Christ's work, not to his divine birth. [3] Valens has intentionally misunderstood the origin of Germinius' creed. He himself abides by the (so-called 'dated') creed drawn up by Mark of Arethusa (at the court at Sirmium, May 22 359), after a long debate at which

Valens was present. That creed, which all signed, said 'like the Father in all things as the holy scriptures teach'. What is the objection to 'like in all things except ingeneracy, in accordance with the scriptures'? Can opponents adduce from the scriptures any degrees of likeness? [4] The letter's transmission and its absence of authenticating signature are explained.

A Summary of Hilary's *Letter to the Emperor Constantius* [= Liber II *Ad Constantium* pp. 197-205]

[1] Hilary has a God-given opportunity to present his case and knows he will receive an unprejudiced hearing. [2] He is a bishop of Gaul in exile, but continuing to exercise his office through his presbyters. He has been falsely accused and is the victim of a faction; false information from a synod has been sent to the Emperor. The Caesar, Julian, knows Hilary's grievance and has had to put up with slander on account of Hilary's exile. A document from Constantius is to hand. The agent of his exile (Saturninus) is present in Constantinople. Constantius and Julian have both been deceived. Hilary is guiltless of any offence injurious to the priesthood or common Christian profession. [3] Hilary proposes to bring the opponent (Saturninus) forward to confess his falsehoods. But Hilary will keep silence on that and speak of the issue of faith. [4] Dispute about the Father, Son and Holy Ghost into whom we are baptized has led to a lamentable proliferation of creeds. [5] Four creeds were published last year, contradicting one another. [6] The absurdities and irreligion of this exposed. [7] Let us return to our baptismal faith and be satisfied with the creed established by a synod of our forebears (sc. the Nicene). 'Improvements' do not improve it. [8] Constantius is to be admired for seeking a truly scriptural creed. Let him permit Hilary to address the synod presently in session and speak to him about the Gospel teaching. The West has its understanding of the Gospel and the faith is not a matter of dialectics. A new creed is unnecessary. [9] The heretics appeal to the Bible but do not understand it. [10] Let Constantius attend to an address which by speaking from the Bible will heal divisions, strengthen the state and promote his own faith, at a time of disquiet for several reasons. [11] Hilary will not enter into the details of his own case now. He wishes to leave with Constantius the message of the Bible texts.

HILARY OF POITIERS *AGAINST VALENS AND URSACIUS*

Book I

[I] *Preface.* /p.98/

1. The apostle Paul, full of the Holy Ghost, speaks thus to the Corinthians: 'But there abide faith, hope and charity' [1 Cor 13:13]. Thus he comprises the great mystery of truth summed up in a threefold disposition of the human consciousness. But he gives us to understand that the rest of things, whether they be functions or gifts [cf. 1 Cor 13:10], on which we now occupy ourselves as best we can, are to be done away with when, with the advent of our Lord Jesus Christ, there is found the perfection of the heavenly court. For when our corruption has been transformed into the glory of eternity, that which is now thought to be of some importance will be of no importance, when store has begun to be set by that which, in its existence, is sempiternal. But the special quality of faith, hope and charity is this: though our bodies pay the debt of death and crumble away, these ever abide and never cease; though all things human are partial, these alone are entire. For 'whether there be prophecies they shall be done away, whether there be tongues they shall cease, whether there be knowledge it shall be destroyed' [1 Cor 13:8.]; but these three higher things attain to an unchanging perfection and will procure nothing from outside nor will they seek greater riches than they possess. For when ultimate truth discards prophecy, tongues and knowledge, eternity itself lays claim to faith, hope and charity, mediators, as they will be, and advocates of the eternity which is apprehended. /p. 99/ The same blessed apostle, indeed, marked out the qualities of other individual things with an indication of their scanty worth, so that it would readily be understood that, with these other things being done away by the progress of heavenly growth, there will be these three which abide by the abundant fruit of their own worth.

2. So, if God is believed by one, who does not know him, to be God, God bestows on him the recompense of righteousness [cf. Heb 11:6]. That is why it is faith which first justifies Abraham [cf. Rom. 4:3, 9], why the faith of the Canaanite mother, trying the Lord in his silence,

saves her daughter [Matt. 15:22-28], and why, in John, power is given
to those who 'believe in his name' to be 'born of God' [cf. John 1:12].
Great is the dignity of faith and those who trust God have a perfect
blessing whereby though born in a body, in iniquity and in sickness,
they have righteousness, health and birth from God. Hope, indeed, is
superior to the delights of earthly life and the goods of a world content
with what it believes God has ordained, foregoing present, to deserve
future, benefits. The Lord endows hope with this reward: 'Everyone
who has left house or brothers or sisters or mother or sons or land for
my name, shall receive a hundredfold and will possess eternal life'
[Matt. 19:29]. Hope, the pre-eminent virtue, God's witness, pledge of
its own expectation! Hope spurns all present things as insecure nothings,
but grasps things to come as eternal and present. Yet though the same
apostle attributes an equal glory to the abiding faith, hope and charity
[cf. 1 Cor. 13:13], and indicates that they are alike imperishable, he
none the less discloses that charity excells the rest. For through charity
we are joined to God by a certain bond of God-given love and our will
becomes inseparable from him once devotion to his name has been
imparted by his charity from which neither sword, nor hunger nor
nakedness will separate us [cf. Rom 8:35], and by which anger, envy,
/p. 100/ ambition, selfishness, extravagance and greed are checked. And
therefore, though there abide faith, hope and charity, the greatest of
these is charity [cf. 1 Cor 13:13]; and no power of worldly disturbances
dissolves or divides those joined through charity in an infrangible love
in God's name.

3. And amongst others (if I have a place after them) I too render my
witness to this so great, so weighty apostolic authority for this charity
laid up for us who have been chosen, ere the world's times, to hope for
heaven. I cleave to the name of the God and Lord Jesus Christ, spurning
the company of the wicked and association with the faithless. With that
association would have been given me, as much as it was to others, a
power to prosper in worldly goods, to enjoy domestic ease, to bask in
all the advantages of pride on familiarity with royalty and of being a
falsely named bishop important in each and every aspect of the Church's
public and private government. These would have been given me, had
I indeed corrupted gospel truth with falsehood, assuaged the guilt of my
conscience with the anodyne of ignorance, defended the corruption of

judgement by the plea of another's will; had I been acquitted of the
stain of heresy by the ingenuousness of the ignorant rather than by my
own creed which was assuredly guilty of it; had I given the lie to
integrity under cover of the difficulty of public knowledge. For these
are things which charity, abiding in simplicity of heart through faith and
hope, did not permit. I had learned from the apostle: 'We have not
received a spirit of fear' [cf. Rom 8:15]; and we have been taught by
the Lord's saying: 'Everyone who shall acknowledge me before men I
too will acknowledge before my Father who is in heaven' [Tim 1:7];
and by the same Lord's words: 'Blessed are they who suffer persecution
for righteousness' sake, since theirs is the kingdom of heaven; blessed
are you, when they curse you and persecute you and say every evil
against you for righteousness' sake; rejoice and be glad, since /p.101/
rich is your reward in heaven' [Matt 5:10-12]. And so I could not prefer
a fawning conscience, silent at guilt, to the endurance of injustice for
the sake of confessing God.

4.[1] I therefore essay to bring to public consciousness a grievous complex
business, beset by devilish deceit, subtle through the involvement of
heretics, prejudiced by the hypocrisy and fear of many, wide ranging in
the dispersal of the regions in which the matter has been transacted and
in which we ourselves have been living; a business ancient in time, new
by its lack of disclosure, passed by previously in a feigned tranquillity
of affairs, most recently renewed by the irreligious cunning of the most
deceitful men. This is the business whereby even in the affairs of the

---

[1] Para. 4: *I therefore...deceit*] Cf. Phoebadius of Agen *Against the Arians* [CPL 473] 1.
ibid.: *a business...men*] Hilary speaks allusively. The hypocritical assent of Valens and
Ursacius in 345 to Athanasius' acquittal (see no. VI) produced a false, deceptive peace
now shattered by a revival of the ancient issue of Athanasius under the regime of
Constantius. ibid.: *bishops travel...*] So also notes Ammianus Marcellinus, the non-
Christian historian, when he speaks about Constantius' policy towards the Church: 'The
plain and simple religion of the Christians he obscured by a dotard's superstition, and by
subtle and involved discussions about dogma, rather than by seriously trying to make them
agree, he aroused many controversies; and as these spread more and more, he fed them
with contentious words. And since throngs of bishops hastened hither and thither on the
public post-horses to the various synods, as they call them, while he sought to make the
whole ritual conform to his own will, he cut the sinews of the courier-service' (*History*,
book XXI 18: translation by J.C. Rolfe in Loeb Classical Library no. 315 Cambridge
Mass./London 1940).
ibid.: *certain of God's priests*] Paulinus (see below, Para. 6), Dionysius of Milan (see
below, no. XI Para. 3, Book Two Para. 4), Eusebius of Vercelli, Lucifer of Cagliari (see
Book Two ibid.) and others perhaps.

Roman empire quiet is being removed, the monarch vexed, the palace agitated; bishops travel hither and yon, attendant magistrates fly about, turmoil besets apostolic men through the general hurry of officialdom. So great is the universal activity, bustle and pressure that the toil and trouble involved in procuring a declaration betray clearly its injustice. Indeed I recollect that it has been a theme of men's discussion for a long time that certain of God's priests are in exile because they object to condemning Athanasius; and such is the error that has taken possession of almost everybody's mind, that they think an exile undertaken for his sake a cause insufficiently worthy of each of them.

5.[1] But I leave aside the fact that though the deepest respect should be paid to the Emperor because, indeed sovereignty comes from God, nevertheless his ruling is not being adopted passively by episcopal judgements, because what belongs to Caesar should be rendered to Caesar but to God what belongs to God [cf. Lk 20:35]. I say nothing of the Emperor's decision to discontinue the examination of the case. I do not complain of a sentence on an absent party being wrung out, although priestly integrity ought not to endure this seeing that the Apostle declares: 'Where faith is, there too is liberty' [cf. 2 Cor 3:17]. But these things I leave aside, not because they are to be disregarded but because weightier matters underly them. For although what was enacted at Biterrae could show that events /p. 102/ happened far otherwise than was supposed, nevertheless I decided to set forth the whole affair in this volume from a weightier concern. For these things were then being hurriedly inflicted upon us: corruption of the gospels, perversion of the faith, hypocritical and blasphemous profession of Christ's name. And in that discussion all things had to be over-hasty, disordered, confused; because the more ample the care with which we

[1] Para. 5: *episcopal judgements*] By Paulinus etc., or perhaps by the bishops in general. ibid.: *Emperor's decision...case*] Smulders (see bibliography) translates: 'cognizance of the case is withheld from him' i.e. Constantius is not permitted as an unbaptized person (he was not baptized till on his deathbed) to intervene in these matters. That may be right, but the above version makes better sense: Constantius considered the matter closed. ibid.:*absent party*] Athanasius. ibid.: *at Biterrae*] Reading with Duchesne *quae Biterris* for *quibusque in terris*, see Smulders' Excursus pp. 88-91. A precise note of place and/or date seems to be required by 'then' in the next sentence.

sought a hearing, the more stubborn was the zeal with which these men resisted that hearing.

6.[1] So I shall begin from events of most recent occurrence, that is to say from the time when first my brother and fellow-minister Paulinus, bishop of Triveri, did not implicate himself at Arles in their ruin and hypocrisy. I shall set forth the sort of decision that was given, a decision he refused to assent to and so was adjudged unworthy of the Church by bishops and worthy of exile by the sovereign. Moreover, it is not history but the interpretation demanded of present circumstances which shows this to be the case: what is to be understood from the events which began the injustice towards someone who did not agree with them is confession of faith rather than personal partiality.

7. And I will give the following important advice: careful attention should be paid to the whole volume. For the matters are all separate in their dates and distinct in their judgements; the different persons involved in them should be noted and the different meanings of the words used, lest perchance the reader be completely nauseated before the end by the quantity of the correspondence and the rapid succession of synods. But we are here concerned with gaining knowledge of God, with the hope of eternity, with him in whom perfect truth adheres. Since a business of so great a weight will be treated of, everyone should bestow care upon understanding these matters, so that standing firm in his own judgement he will not thereafter follow someone else's opinion.

---

[1] Para. 6: *Moreover...*] 'You can see from what has hapened in the case of Paulinus, what you could not see by merely recounting the events, that Christian faith, not indulgence towards Athanasius, is the issue'.

[II] /p. 48/ *Decree[1] of the synod of Eastern bishops on the Arian side at Sardica, sent by them to Africa.*

[2]Everlasting salvation in the Lord to Gregory bishop of Alexandria, to Amfion bishop of Nicomedia, Donatus bishop of Carthage, Desiderius bishop, of Campania, Fortunatus bishop of Neapolis in Campania, Euthicius bishop of Campania, the clergy of Rimini, Maximus bishop of Salona in Dalmatia, Sinferon, and all our fellow-bishops, priests and deacons throughout the world, and to all bishops under heaven in the /p. 49/ holy Catholic Church, from us, who met together from the various provinces of the East (viz. the province of the Thebaid, the province of Palestine, from Arabia, Foenicia, Syria, Mesopotamia, Cilicia, Isauria, Cappadocia, Galacia, Pontus, Bitinia, Pamphilia, Paflagonia, Caria, Frigia, Pisidia and the islands of the Ciclades, Lidia, Asia, Europe, the Hellespont, Trachia, Emimontus) at the town of Serdica and held a council.

1. It is, indeed, beloved brethren, the constant prayer of us all: first, that the Lord's holy Catholic Church should be free of all dissensions and schisms and should everywhere preserve the unity of the Spirit and the bond of charity through upright faith (and, indeed, all who invoke the Lord, especially we who are bishops in charge of most holy churches, ought also to hold, embrace, guard and keep spotless our life); secondly, that the rule of the Church and the sacred tradition and judgements of our forebears should remain firm and solid, and that no disturbance should at any time be caused by newly emerging sects and perverse teachings, especially in appointments and dismissals of bishops, as a result of which the Church would fail to maintain evangelical and sacred

---

[1] Heading: *Decree...Africa*] Heading presumably by the excerptor. The document survives, in what is apparently Hilary's translation, only here. 'Arian' is, of course, not the self-description of the authors: nobody claimed to follow him, though some (certainly not these) thought him wrongly condemned. The date of the Council is not certain. If we accept the evidence of the Index to Athanasius' *Festal Letters* [CPG 2102], it is 343. If that of a notice in the Codex Veronensis 60 (edited Cuthbert Turner *Ecclesiae occidentalis monumenta iuris antiquissima* (Oxford, 1899ff Tome I part 2 p.637), as emended by Eduard Schwartz from the impossible *Constantini et Constantinis* to read *Constantii III et Constantis II*, the date will be 342. Brennecke (see bibliography) pp. 27 - 29 explains the issue and chooses 342.The letter was evidently sent to Carthage for transmission to the rest.

[2] Salutation: *Gregory*] 'Intruder' at Alexandria 339 - 346.

instructions ordered by the holy and most blessed apostles and by our
forebears, instructions which have been kept, and are being kept, secure
by us up to the present day.

2.[1] For in our days there has arisen a certain Marcellus of Galacia, a
more abominable plague than all the other heretics, one who with
sacrilegious mind, profane mouth and incorrigible argumentativeness
means to limit the Lord Christ's everlasting, eternal and timeless reign,
saying that the Lord's reign had a beginning 400 years ago and will
have its end at the same time as the world's setting [cf. 1 Cor 15:24f].
/p. 50/ He attempts also, in the audacity of his venture, to maintain that
the Lord Christ became the 'image of the invisible God' [cf. Col 1:15]
at the conception of his body and that it was then too that he was made
'bread' [Jn 6:48] 'door' [Jn 10:7] and 'life' [Jn 1:4]. Moreover, it is not
only this that he affirms in words and verbose assertion but the sum of
whatever was conceived by sacrilegious mind and uttered by
blaspheming mouth. With huge audacity he even puts down in a book
replete with blasphemies and abominations other, far worse things,
against Christ, slandering him by using his perverse mind to attach to
the divine scriptures things opposed to them along with his own
interpretation and misrepresenatation of them. From which it is manifest
and clear that he is a heretic. Mingling his own assertions with certain
foulnesses (sometimes with Sabellius' falsehoods, sometimes with Paul
of Samosata's mischief, sometimes with the blasphemies of Montanus
the leader of all the heretics) and making a single medley of the
aforesaid, he has, like the foolish Galatian [Gal 3:1f] he is, turned aside
to another gospel which is not another gospel according to what the
blessed apostle Paul says when he condemns such people: 'Even if an
angel from heaven should proclaim to us otherwise than you have
received, let him be anathema' [Gal 1:8f].

---

[1] **Para. 2:** *Marcellus*] See, most conveniently, Hanson (see bibliography) pp. 217 -235.
Ejected from his see for his theology (much subtler than, but just as provocative as, the
caricature of it which follows suggests) in 336 (or 335). The line in the 'Nicene' creed,
of his kingdom there will be no end, owes its place there to him: an exclusive clause, it
occurs in synodical creeds from 341 (the Council of Antioch) onwards.

3.[1] Great was the concern of our forebears and predecessors over the above mentioned sacrilegious preaching. A council of bishops, indeed, was summoned to Constantinople in the presence of the Emperor Constantine of most blessed memory. They came from many of the Eastern provinces to set right a man imbued with evils and so that he, admonished by their most sacred censure, might depart from his sacrilegious preaching. They rebuked him and upbraided him, /p. 51/ expostulating with him in a spirit of charity for a long time, and made no progress at all. For when they had failed to make progress after a first, a second and repeated censures (for he was obstinate, he gainsaid the correct faith and withstood the Catholic Church with spiteful opposition) they then began to abhor and shun him. They saw how he had been laid low by sin and was self-damned, and condemned him by ecclesiastical proceedings, lest he should further taint the Church's sheep by his evil, pestilential touch. Then, indeed, they also stored in the church's archives certain of his most depraved thoughts against correct faith and most holy Church, to be a reminder to posterity and a precaution for their own most sacred scriptures. But these were the first impieties of Marcellus the heretic; worse then ensued. For what faithful soul would credit or endure his evil deeds and writings which have been fittingly anathematized already along with himself by our fathers at Constantinople? A volume of judgements against him, jointly written by the bishops, is, indeed, extant, and even those who are now on Marcellus' side and support him (i.e. Protogenes, bishop of Sardica, and Cyriacus from Naisus) joined in writing down a judgement in this book against him with their own hand. Their powerful hand bears witness that the most holy faith is not to be changed in any manner nor is holy Church to be laid low by false preaching, lest in this way a disease and pestilence of souls most grievous to men should be introduced. As Paul says: 'Whether we, or an angel from heaven, should preach to you otherwise than you have received, let him be anathema' [Gal 1:9].

---

[1] Para. 3: *..to Constantinople*] Probably in 336. Eusebius of Caesarea, writing against Marcellus (*Against Marcellus* II, 4 [58]) apparently refers to this condemnation here. Sozomen *(History of the Church* [CPG 6030] II, 33) speaks of previous arraignments at Jerusalem and Tyre.
ibid.: *..volume of judgements*] The judges' decision together with their signatures.

4. However, we are extremely surprised at the extent to which certain persons /p. 52/ who wish to be churchmen are readily receiving into communion this man who ventures to preach the gospel otherwise than it is in truth; they do not enquire into his blasphemies as designated in his own book, and have refused to reach a common mind with those who have carefully investigated them all and on detecting them have justly condemned him. For though Marcellus was considered a heretic amongst his own people, he sought out means to travel abroad; in order, that is, to deceive those who were unaware of him and his pestilential writings. But in all his behaviour amongst them he has taken advantage of the naive and guileless, hiding his own impious writings and profane opinions and putting forward falsehoods instead of the truth. Under cover of Church law he has deluded many of the Church's pastors and got them under his control, deceiving them with a cunning fraud, introducing the doctrines of Sabellius the heretic and renewing the schemes and tricks of Paul of Samosata. The outlandish teaching of Marcellus is, indeed, a medley of all the heresies, as we mentioned above. For that reason it would have been as well for all in charge of holy Church to remember the Lord Christ's words: 'Beware of false prophets, who approach you in sheep's clothing but are ravening wolves within; you shall know them by their fruits'.[1] They should shun such people and abhor them, should not readily enter into communion with them, should recognize them by their actions and condemn them beforehand on the basis of their sacrilegious writings. We are now very afraid that the scripture may be fulfilled in our days which says: 'When men were asleep there came the enemy and sowed tares among the corn' [Matt 13:25]. For when those whose duty it is to keep watch over the Church are not awake, falsehood imitates truth and utterly subverts right.

5. And so we, who are fully cognizant, on the basis of Marcellus's book, of his doctrines and crimes, write to you, very dear brethren, to warn you not to admit to the fellowship of holy Church either Marcellus or his partisans, and to be mindful of the prophet David /p. 53/ when he says: 'I have said to those who do wrong "do no wrong", and to those

---

[1] Matt 7:15f.

who offend "do not lift up your horn on high, do not speak iniquities
against God" [Ps 75 (74):5]. Believe Solomon when he says 'Do not
remove the everlasting landmarks which your fathers set up' [Prov
22:28]. These things being so, do not follow the errors of the aforesaid
most depraved Marcellus. Condemn the things he has invented and
taught against the Lord Christ with his wrongful preaching, beforehand,
lest you yourselves be partners in his blasphemies and wickednesses. So
much by way of summary on Marcellus!

6.[1] But in the case of Athanasius, formerly bishop of Alexandria, you
are to understand what was enacted. He was charged with the grave
offence of sacrilege and profanation of holy Church's sacraments. With
his own hands he split a chalice consecrated to God and Christ, broke
down the august altar itself, overturned the bishop's throne and razed
the basilica itself, God's house, Christ's church, to the ground. The
presbyter himself, an earnest and upright man called Scyras, he
delivered to military custody. In addition to this, Athanasius was
charged with unlawful acts, with the use of force, with murder and the
killing of bishops. Raging like a tyrant even during the most holy days
of Easter and accompanied by the military and officials of the imperial
government who, on his authority, confined some to custody, beat and
whipped some and forced the rest into sacrilegious communion with
him, by various acts of torture (innocent men would never have behaved
so!) Athanasius hoped that in this way his own people and his own
faction would get the upper hand; and so he forced unwilling people
into communion by means of military officials, judges, prisons,
whippings and various acts of torture, compelled recusants and browbeat
those who fought back and withstood him. Serious and painful, indeed,
were the charges laid against him by the accusers.

---

[1] Para. 6: *Athanasius*] Church discipline, not doctrine (save by association with
Marcellus) is in question here. Cf. what is said here with III Para. 5 below: no allegation
of murder here. For contemporary evidence of Athanasius' violence see H. I. Bell *Jews
and Christians in Egypt* (1934).

7.[1] /p. 54/ For these reasons it was thought necessary for a council to be convened: in the first instance at Caesarea in Palestine, but when neither he nor any of his entourage turned up to the aforesaid council, it had to be repeated, owing to his misdemeanours, a year later at Tyre. Bound by a decree of the Emperor, bishops arrived from Macedonia, Pannonia, Bithynia and all parts of the East. They took knowledge in their proceedings of Athanasius' immoral and criminal acts and did not give a general and hasty credence to the accusers; they chose distinguished and well-regarded bishops and despatched them to the actual place at which the things, complained of against Athanasius, had happened. The bishops viewed everything with their very eyes, took note of the true facts and on returning to the council confirmed, with their own testimony, that the criminal offences he was charged on by the accusers were true. And so they passed on Athanasius, present in person, a sentence appropriate to his offences. That was why he fled Tyre and appealed to the Emperor. The Emperor heard him, and after questioning him recognized all his misdemeanours and sentenced him to banishment. Events having turned out thus, the authority of the law has been maintained by all the bishops in their repudiation of wrongdoings, as have the Church's canons and the holy teaching of the apostles: since Athanasius was duly condemned and deservedly exiled for his misdeeds as a sacrilegious person, a profaner of the holy sacraments, as guilty of violence in the destruction of a basilica, as a man to be abhorred for the deaths of bishops and the harassment of guiltless brethren.

8.[2] But seeing that Athanasius after his condemnation had procured himself a return from exile, he arrived back in Alexandria from Gaul after a fair length of time. Reckless of the past he became harsher in villainy. His first acts are trivialities compared with what followed. Throughout the course of his journey back he was subverting the churches: some condemned bishops he restored, /p. 55/ to some he held out the hope of a return to episcopal office, some pagans he ordained bishop although there were bishops who had stayed sound and whole

---

[1] Para. 7: *Caesarea*] Eusebius, not wholly unsympathetic to Arius, was its bishop, of course.
ibid.: *they chose...happened*] Often called the 'Mareotic Commission'. Its members included Valens and Ursacius.

[2] Para. 8: *time*] On November 23rd 337.

throughout the murderous attacks of the gentiles; heedless of the laws, he set all his store by foolhardiness. So it was that he despoiled the basilicas of Alexandria, by violence, by lethal attack, by a campaign. Though a holy and sound bishop had been appointed in his stead by the decision of the council, he, like a barbarian enemy, like a sacrilegious plague, set fire to God's temple with the peoples of the gentiles on hand, broke the altar and secretly, clandestinely, made his escape in exile from the city.

9.[1] Anyone who hears about Paul, formerly bishop of Constantinople, after Paul's return from exile, will be horrified.. /lacuna/ ..There took place, indeed, also at Anquira, in the province of Galatia, after Marcellus the heretic's return, house-burnings and various kinds of aggressive act. He dragged naked presbyters into the forum and (to be mentioned with tears and lamentation!) openly and publicly profaned the consecrated body of the Lord hanging round the bishops' necks. Holy virgins vowed to God and Christ, their clothes dragged off, he exposed with horrifying foulness in the forum and the city centre to the gathered populace. In the city of Gaza, in the province of Palestine, Asclepas after his return smashed the altar and caused many riots. In addition to this, at Adrianopolis, Lucius, after his return ordered (if it be not wrong even to mention such a thing) that the sacrifice prepared by holy and sound bishops should be thrown to the dogs. Therefore, these things being so, shall we go so far as to entrust Christ's sheep to such great wolves? Shall we make Christ's members, members of a harlot? [1 Cor 6:15]. God forbid!

10. Subsequently, Athanasius roamed the various parts of the world, misleading some and deceiving guileless bishops ignorant of his trickery

---

[1]Para. 9: *Paul*] Elected probably in 332, he was a signatory to Athanasius' deposition at Tyre and himself deposed about four years later. He returned to his see on Constantine's death but was deposed again in 338, to return in 341 on the death of the 'intruder', another Eusebius (see below Para. 20).
ibid.: *Asclepas*] He was deposed 17 years before (see Para. 11) = 326 or 327. He returned in 337, to be removed again. He joined Athanasius in 340, went back to his see c. 347 and died c. 355.
ibid.: *Lucius*] Deposed in the late 320s, he returned in 337. He was deposed after Serdica but returned in 347. He evidently took the view that the unworthiness of the minister invalidates the sacrament.

and pestilential flattery, even some Egyptian bishops unaware of his activities. /p. 56/ He disturbed churches at peace or arbitrarily fabricated new churches for himself at will by soliciting subscriptions from individuals. However, this could have no effect with regard to the judgement much earlier given sacred force by the holy and distinguished bishops. For the commendation of those who were not judges in the council and never had the council's judgement and are known not to have been present when the aforesaid Athanasius was heard, could have no validity nor could it profit him. Finally, when he recognized that these things had been of no avail, he went off to Julius in Rome and to certain Italian bishops of his own party as well. He deceived them by the falsehood of his letters and they received him quite readily into communion. Thereupon they began to be in difficulty not so much over him as over their own actions, because they had believed him rashly and communicated with him. For if these were letters from certain people, neverthless they were not from those who had either been judges or had sat at the council. Indeed, even had they been certain people's letters, they ought never to have rashly trusted this spokesman in his own cause.

11. But the judges who pronounced a fitting sentence upon him, refused to believe him, for this reason: certain others, exposed in the past for their misdemeanours (we mean Asclepas, deprived of episcopal honour 17 years ago, Paul, Lucius and all who joined such people) joined with Marcellus and Athanasius. Together they toured foreign parts and persuaded people not to believe the judges who rightly condemned them, in order that, by this kind of traffic, they might sometime procure themselves a return to episcopal office. They did not put their case in the places where they had sinned, or even close to where they had accusers, but amongst foreigners living a long way from their countries /p. 57/ with no reliable knowledge of the facts. They attempted to cancel the just sentence by referring their own actions for reconsideration by people entirely ignorant of them. This was cunning of them. They knew that a large number of the judges, accusers and witnesses had died, and they hoped to secure a retrial after so many important judgements, meaning to plead their cause before us who have neither acquitted nor condemned them. For those who had tried the case have gone to the Lord.

12.[1] But they also wanted to plead their cause to Eastern bishops even, and so defenders appear instead of judges, accused instead of defenders, at a time when defence by these was of no avail, principally because they could not be defended when their own accusers denounced them face to face. They hoped to bring in a new law: that Eastern bishops should be tried by Western. They wanted the Church's judgement to be capable of being established by people who took pity not so much on *their* actions as on their own. So, because church rules of government have never accepted this wrong principle, we ask you, dear brethren, yourselves to condemn along with us those wicked and deadly destructive efforts on the part of lost souls.

13. Indeed, when Athanasius was still bishop, he himself condemned the deposed Asclepas by his own judgement. Marcellus likewise never communicated with him. Paul, on the other hand, was present at Athanasius' deposition and himself wrote down the sentence, along with the rest, and condemned him, in his own hand. So long as each of them was bishop, he confirmed his own judgements. But when for various reasons and at various times each of them was deservedly and duly expelled from the Church, with one accord they effected a larger alliance by each of them pardoning himself faults which, when they were bishops, they had condemned on divine authority.

14.[2] Now since Athanasius, on his travels to Italy and Gaul, had gained himself a trial after the death of some of the accusers, witnesses and judges, and was hoping to be heard again at a time when his misdemeanours would be obscured by the length of time /p. 58/ (Julius, bishop of Rome, Maximinus, Ossius and several others improperly favoured him with their assent and assumed that a council of themselves would take place by courtesy of the Emperor at Serdica), we were convened by the Emperor's letter and arrived at Serdica. On our arrival

---

[1]Para. 12: ..*that Eastern bishops ...Western.*] This is the bone of contention. Canon 3 of the Western half of the Council enshrines the right of appeal to Rome anticipated by Julius in his acquittal of Athanasius and Marcellus. These canons, later annexed to those of Nicaea, were to become normative, at least in the West.

[2]Para. 14.: *Ossius*] He was an important figure prominent throughout this period in councils, appearing in our texts elsewhere. He had been the chief bishop present at Nicea (325), presided now at Serdica, and was a supporter of Athanasius until he gave way under pressure from the Emperor Constantius (see Book Three no. II)

we learned that Athanasius, Marcellus and all the villains expelled by a council's judgement and deservedly condemned beforehand, each one for his misdeeds, were sitting together in discussion with Ossius and Protogenes in the middle of the church and (what is worse) celebrating the divine mysteries. Nor was Protogenes, bishop of Serdica, embarrassed by communion with Marcellus the heretic, whose sect and abominable views he had himself condemned in council with his own voice four times subscribing to the bishops' judgements. From this it is clear that he has condemned himself by his own judgement, since he has made himself a partner with him by communicating with him.

15. We, though, holding to the discipline of the Church's rule and wanting to help the wretches to some extent, enjoined those accompanying Protogenes and Ossius, to exclude the condemned men from their assembly and not to communicate with sinners. They were to listen, along with us, to the judgements pronounced against them by our fathers in the past. For Marcellus' book requires no formal accusation (he is self-evidently a heretic). They were not to heed false suggestions, for each of them made his depraved meaning opaque for the sake of the post of bishop. But they opposed this, for some unknown reason; and refusing to withdraw from communion with them, they confirmed Marcellus the heretic's teaching, Athanasius' misdeeds and the misdemeanours of the rest, preferring them to the Church's faith and peace.

16. So when this was known, we 80 bishops, who had come to Serdica with huge labour and toil from various distant provinces, for the sake of establishing the Church's peace, could not endure the sight without tears. For it was no light matter that they absolutely refused to rid themselves of people whom our fathers /p. 59/ had previously condemned for their offences. So we thought it wrong to communicate with them and did not choose to share the Lord's holy sacraments with profane people, preserving and keeping, as we do, the discipline of the Church's rule. For it may be that it was from a bad conscience that they did not rid themselves of the aforesaid Ossius and Protogenes: because each of them was afraid of being left defenceless, and they greatly dreaded this happening publicly. Thus none of them dared pronounce sentence against them for fear he should condemn himself too for

having communicated, contrary to the ban, with people he ought in no way to have communicated with.

17. We, for our part, repeatedly asked them not to shake firm and solid principles, not to overthrow law or disturb divine injunctions, not to confound everything and render even a modest portion of the Church's tradition empty, nor also to bring in a new doctrine or to prefer in some particular Western to Eastern bishops and most sacred councils. But our opponents disregarded this and threatened us, promising that they would vindicate Athanasius and the rest of the miscreants. As if, indeed, people who had taken into their company all miscreants and lost souls could do or say aught else! Moreover, they put this forward with enormous vanity, possessed by headstrong foolhardiness rather than right reason. For they saw that those who receive condemned people incur a charge of wrongdoing as violators of heaven's laws, and they tried to constitute a court of such weight that they would like to call themselves judges of judges and reopen the decision (if that can rightly be done) of those now with God. We asked them over many days to cast aside condemned people, unite with holy Church and concur with fathers who spoke true. They absolutely refused to do so.

18.[1] /p. 60/ While, therefore, we were engaged in argument, there came forward five bishops from our side, survivors of the six who had been despatched to Mareotis. They put forward to them the option of sending some bishops from both councils to the places where Athanasius had committed his offences and outrages, and they would write down all the things faithfully on oath; if what we had announced to the council were false inventions, we ourselves would be condemned and would not complain to the Emperors or to any council or bishop. But if what we had previously said was established truth, we should depose 'those of you whom you have selected, up to our number' i.e., those who communicated with Athanasius after his condemnation including those who are supporters and defenders of Athanasius and Marcellus; and they 'should not complain in any way to the Emperors, a council or any

---

[1]Para 18: *..five bishops...survivors of the six...*] The original six were: Theognis/Theognitus of Nicea, Maris of Chalcedon, Ursacius, Valens, Theodorus of Heraclea, and Mac(h)edonius of Mopsuestia. Theognis had since died.

bishop of yours'. Ossius, Protogenes and all their allies were frightened of taking up our proposed option.

19. A vast multitude, all of them vicious and abandoned souls, converged upon Serdica, arriving from Constantinople and Alexandria. Then people guilty of murder, guilty of manslaughter, guilty of violence, guilty of robbery, guilty of looting, guilty of despoliation, guilty of all unspeakable sacrileges and crimes; people who have broken down altars, set fire to churches and plundered the houses of private citizens, profanators of God's mysteries and betrayers of Christ's sacraments; who oppose the Church's faith and make the impious and wicked doctrine of the heretics their own and have slaughtered God's wisest presbyters, deacons and bishops in hideous carnage. All these Ossius and Protogenes have gathered together with them in their little assembly. They honoured these and disdained all of us deacons and priests of God, because we refused ever to join with such people. They reported our private business to the general public and to all the heathen, /p. 61/ fabricating lies instead of the truth and telling the tale of a disagreement arising not from grounds of religion but from human arrogance. They confused things human and divine, connected private matters with Church matters and confounded harmony with us and disorder in the city, by saying we should bring heavy damage upon the city unless we communicated with them (which was unlawful). This was their repeated cry. For we have absolutely refused to communicate with them unless they expel those we have condemned and award the council of the East its fitting esteem.

20.[1] From the following you can learn what they themselves did and the kind of council they held. Protogenes, as we said above, anathematized in the proceedings Marcellus and Paul, but afterwards received them into communion. Yet they had in their council Dionisius of Elida in the province of Acaia, whom they had themselves deposed. Deposers and deposed, judges and guilty accused, communicate and celebrate with them together the divine mysteries. They ordained as bishop Bassus, from Diocletianopolis, who had been detected in disgraceful acts of

---

[1]Para. 20: *proceedings*] I.e. in the business and the records of it.

wrongdoing and deservedly banished from Syria. Caught out in even
more disgraceful life amongst them, and though condemned by them,
he appears today as united with them. Protogenes made frequent charges
of many lewd acts and crimes against Aëtius of Tessalonica, saying that
Aëtius had, and has, concubines; and refused ever to communicate with
him. Now, however, taken back into amity, as if cleared by association
with worse people, he is thought of amongst them as an honest man.
Asclepas, when he had come to Constantinople on account of Paul, after
the barbarity and savagery of the things he committed, things done in
the midst of the church of Constantinople, after a thousand murders,
which stained the altars themselves with human blood, after the killings
of brethren and annihilations of pagans, today does not cease to
communicate with Paul, the cause of these events, and neither do they:
they communicate with Paul through Asclepas, receiving letters from
Paul and sending letters to Asclepas.

21. /p. 62/ What sort of council, made up of this curdled blend of lost
souls, could be solemnized - a council at which they do not punish, so
much as acknowledge, their own misdeeds? Not so with us who preside
over holy churches and are guides to lay-people, we who pardon and
forgive what they themselves could never pardon or forgive. These have
forgiven even Marcellus, Athanasius and the rest of the villains,
impieties and blasphemies which it was wrong to pardon, since it is
written: 'If man sins against man, they will pray for him to the Lord;
but if man sins against God, who will pray for him?' [1 Sam 2:25].
'But we have no such custom, nor has God's Church' [1 Cor 11:16].
We allow nobody to teach these things or to import new teachings, lest
we be called traitors to the faith and betrayers of the divine scriptures,
a wrong for which we would be condemned by the Lord and by men.

22. But the aforesaid people contrived these schemes against us, and
because they knew we could not aid wicked people by communicating
with them, thought to frighten us with the Emperors' letters and so drag
us unwillingly into their fellowship; they saw the deep and everlasting
peace of the whole world and Church sundered because of Athanasius
and Marcellus through whom God's name is being blasphemed amongst
the gentiles [cf. Rom 2:24 (Is 52:5)]. They ought, if they had any fear
of God that this tumult generated by themselves would last, to depart,

even at this late stage, from their most depraved arrogance, lest the Church be rent asunder because of them. Or if, amongst those who maintain their own cause, there be the fear of God, though nothing deserving condemnation be found with them, nevertheless because the unity of the Church is being rent owing to them and deep peace overturned owing to a mad and furious lust for honour, they ought to abominate and hold in horror those people.

23. /p.63/ When we saw things taking this course, each of us decided to go back to his own country; we decided to write from Serdica, tell what happened and express our judgement. For we could not take back into the status of bishop Athanasius and Marcellus, who have led wicked lives and blasphemed against the Lord, men deposed and condemned some time ago. These men have 'crucified the Son of God and put him to open shame' [Heb 6:6], piercing him with biting thrusts. For one of them, by blaspheming against the Son of God and his everlasting reign [cf. Lk 1:33], is dead once and for all. The other, committed atrocious sin by his profane conduct towards the Lord's body and his sacraments, and did other monstrous misdeeds. He was expelled and condemned by sentence of bishops. For this reason, since we cannot depart from the teaching of our forebears because the Church has not assumed such authority nor received such power from God, we ourselves too do not admit the aforesaid to the Church's honour and dignity and those who do admit them we rightly condemn. Nor do we accept in Church others deservedly condemned either some time ago or latterly. We stick to God's laws, our fathers' teachings and the Church's instructions, believing, as we do, the prophet who says: 'Do not pass over the everlasting boundaries which your fathers set down' [Prov 22; 28]. That is why we will never disturb what is fixed and solid, but will preserve, rather, what our forebears have established.

24. Therefore, very dear brethren, with much behind us, we give you the open command that none of you is ever to be cajoled into communion with Ossius, Protogenes, Athanasius, Marcellus, Asclepas, Paul or Julius; nor with any of those condemned and expelled from holy Church or with associates of theirs who communicate with them either in person or by letters. For that reason you ought never to write to them or receive letters from them. It remains for us to bid you, /p. 64/ very

dear brethren, take thought for the unity of the Church and its perpetual peace, and select holy bishops in whom there is both a sound faith and holy life, and that you hold in horror people deprived of episcopal status for their crimes who want to get back a position they rightly forfeited for their offences. Abominate more and more the people you see committing worse and worse offences, heedless, as they are, of the Lord who says: 'You have sinned? do it no more' [cf. Ecclus 21:1.; Jn 5:14]. For they swagger and become stronger with their misdeeds and sink into all the greater an abyss of vices the more they subvert the whole world. With time to spend on quarrels they wage wars of bitter persecution on the holy churches and fight, like usurpers, to make God's people captives under their control.

25. Recognize, from these facts, indeed, their most evil endeavours when they had brought such a tempestuous squall upon the world as to trouble almost the whole of the East and West with it. The result was that each of us left behind church duties, abandoned God's people and neglected the very teaching of the Gospel in order to come here from afar, old men, as we are, heavy with age, weak in body, feeble and ill (we were dragged through different places, we left our sick behind on the roads, for the sake of a very few villains rightly condemned long ago who unlawfully desired to be heads of the Church) and that the government too concerned itself with us: the religious Emperors, the tribunes and high officers were exercised with the dreadful public business arising from the life and condition of the bishops. Nor are the lay-people quiet. All the brotherhood in all the provinces is in suspense, anxiously awaiting the outcome of this storm of ills. The public post is worn to nothing. Why say more? The world, from East to West, is brought to utter ruin over one or two scoundrels of impious views and foul life, and is being disturbed by a severe and violent tempest over people in whom no seeds of religion have remained. If they had any seeds of religion, they would have imitated the prophet /p. 65/ when he says: 'Take me up and throw me into the sea and the sea will be calmed by you, because this tempest has been created on my account' [Jonah 1:12]. But they do not imitate these words, because they do not follow the just. The arch-scoundrels desire headship of the Church as if it were a usurper's kingdom.

26.[1] Nor do they make this enquiry for the benefit of justice. For those who attempt to annul divine judgements and the decisions of others have no consideration for the churches. That is why they have been at pains to import the novelty repugnant to the Church's ancient custom: that whatever Eastern bishops had decided in council could be treated of anew by Western bishops, and likewise anything decided by Western bishops could be annulled by Easterns. Their own depraved view led them to this practice. But the conduct of our predecessors certifies that the rulings of all duly and legally enacted councils are to be confirmed. For the council taking place at Rome in the time of the heretics Novatus, Sabellius and Valentinus was confirmed by the Easterns. And again, what was determined in the East in the time of Paul of Samosata was ratified by all. For this reason we urge you, very dear brethren, to bear in mind the system of Church discipline and to take thought for the peace of the whole world. Censure those who communicate with scoundrels, cut evil people off from the churches by the roots, so that the Lord Christ may float upon the hastening tempest they caused, may bid all the winds and storms of sea depart and bestow on holy Church peace everlasting and calm [Matt 8:26f and parallels].

27.[2] We, for our part, have wronged nobody, but maintain the rulings of the law. We have been gravely wronged and treated ill by those who wanted to trouble the rule of Church discipline by their own wickedness. Having the fear of God before our eyes [cf. Rom 3:18] and Christ's true and just judgement in mind, we have shown bias to none and have not refrained from preserving Church discipline in every case. Accordingly /p. 66/ the whole council condemned, by most ancient law, Julius of Rome, Ossius, Protogenes, Gaudentius and Maximinus of Triveri, as originators of communion with Marcellus, Athanasius and the rest of the scoundrels, and as having even shared in Paul of Constantinople's murders and bloody acts. Protogenes is anathematized

---

[1]Para. 26: ..*council* ...*Valentinus*] Probably a piece of historical myth. The 'heretics' do not belong to the same period (Valentinus, the gnostic, belongs to the middle years of the second century; Novatus (if they do not mean Novatian) to a century later; with Sabellius, if we know anything about him, somewhere in between). So one contemporary council could not have condemned them. The next case adduced, Paul of Samosata, is actual but does not help the Easterns' argument.

[2] Para. 27: ..*because*...*Gaul*] In 342, to invite Constans to help break the deadlock between East and West: see Introduction ii (b) p.xix.

along with Marcellus for subscribing frequently to the sentence brought against Marcellus or his book; they also gave sentence against Paul of Constantinople but afterwards comunicated with him. Gaudentius is anathematized as oblivious of his predecessor Cyriacus who subscribed the sentences rightly brought against the scoundrels and as implicated in the crimes of Paul whom he defended shamelessly. Julius of Rome as chief leader of the villains and the first to open the door to the condemned scoundrels; as one who gave the rest access to an annulling of the divine judgements and who defended Athanasius presumptuously and boldly, Athanasius, neither whose witnesses nor whose accusers he knew. Ossius, for the aforesaid reason and on account of Marcus of blessed memory upon whom he always inflicted grave wrongs and also for having used all his powers to defend all the villains rightly condemned for their crimes and for having lived in the East with abandoned scoundrels; indeed, it was disgraceful of him to be an inseparable friend of Paulinus of Dacia, formerly a bishop, a man who after first being accused of magic and expelled from the Church, lives still to the present day in public apostasy with concubines, fornicating with strumpets, a man whose books of spells were burned by Macedonius, bishop and confessor, of Mopsus. He also acted very wickedly in sticking to Eustasius and Quimatius, as a bosom friend of people whose notorious and disgraceful life is unmentionable; their departure from it has made them known to all. Ossius linked himself with such people from the outset and always encouraged scoundrels; he attacked the Church and always aided and abetted God's foes. Maximinus of Triveri, /p. 67/ because he would not receive our episcopal colleagues, whom we had sent to Gaul and for his being the first to communicate with Paul of Constantinople, a nefarious man and lost soul; also because he was the cause of so much damage that Paul, owing to whom many murders were committed, was recalled to Constantinople. The cause, therefore, of so much murder, was himself the one who recalled Paul, condemned a good while before, to Constantinople.

28. For these reasons, then, the Council considered it right to depose and condemn Julius of Rome, Ossius and the rest of the aforesaid. These things being so, you ought to guard yourselves and abstain from contact with them, very dear brethren, and ought never to admit them to

communion with you; nor should you receive their letters or give letters of recommendation for them. And because Ossius' associates have intended to infringe catholic and apostolic faith by introducing the novel doctrine of Marcellus who has united with Judaism (a novel doctrine which is a judaizing compound of Sabellius and Paul), we have, of necessity, set down the faith of the Catholic Church denied by the aforesaid associates of Ossius who have introduced instead Marcellus the heretic's. It follows that when you have received our letter you should each accord your agreement with this sentence and ratify our decisions with your personal subscription.

Our faith is as follows /p.69/:
29.[1] We believe in one God the Father Almighty, founder and creator of all things, from whom every creature in heaven and earth is named.

And in his Only-begotten Son our Lord Jesus Christ, who was begotten from the Father before eternity, God from God, light from light, through whom were made all things in heaven and on earth, visible and invisible, the Word who is also Wisdom, power, life and true light, who in the last days, for our sake, put on man, was born of the blessed Virgin Mary, crucified, died and was buried. The third day he rose from the dead, and, assumed into heaven, sits on the Father's right, and he will come at the world's end to judge living and dead and to reward each according to his works, and his kingdom lasts without cessation for ever and ever, for he is seated at the Father's right, not only in this age but in the age to come.

We believe in the Holy Ghost, that is the Paraclete, whom he promised to the apostles and sent after his assumption into heaven, /p. 72/ to teach them and instruct them about all things, and through the Holy Ghost are hallowed souls believing rightly in the Son. We believe also in the holy Church, the forgiveness of sin, the resurrection of the flesh, in eternal life.

But those who say the Son is 'out of what was not' or that he is of another substance and not from God, or who say that there was ever time or age when the Son was not: these the holy and Catholic Church condemns as heretics. Likewise those who say there are three Gods; or

---

[1] Para. 29.: *Here ends...*] Excerptor's, or scribe's, note.

that Christ is not God /p. 73/; or that Christ did not exist before eternity and was not Son of God; or that the Father himself and Son and Holy Ghost did not exist before eternity, or that the Son was not born, or that God the Father did not beget the Son by decision and will: all these the holy and Catholic Church anathematizes and execrates.

/p. 74/

Stephen bishop of Antioch in the province of Coele-Syria, I pray you may have good health in the Lord.

Olympius bishop of Doliche, I pray you may have good health in the Lord.

Gerontius bishop of Raphania, I pray you may have good health in the Lord.

Menofantus bishop of Ephesus, I pray you may have good health in the Lord.

Paul bishop, I pray you may have good health in the Lord.

Eulalius bishop of Amasias, I pray you may have good health in the Lord.

Machedonius bishop of Mopsuestia, I pray you may have good health in the Lord.

Thelafius bishop of Calchedonia, I pray you may have good health in the Lord.

Acacius bishop of Caesarea, I pray you may have good health in the Lord.

Theodorus bishop of Heraclia, I pray you may have good health in the Lord.

Quintianus bishop of Gaza, I pray you may have good health in the Lord.

Marcus bishop of Aretusa, I pray you may have good health in the Lord. /p. 75/

Cyrotus bishop of Rosus, I pray you may have good health in the Lord.

Eugeus bishop of Lisinia, I pray you may have good health in the Lord.

Antonius bishop of Zeuma, I pray you may have good health in the Lord.

Antonius bishop of Docimium, I pray you may have good health in the Lord.

Dianius bishop of Caesarea, I pray you may have good health in the Lord.

Vitalis bishop of Tyre, I pray you may have good health in the Lord.
Eudoxius bishop of Germanicia, I pray you may have good health in the Lord.
Dionisius bishop of Alexandria in the province of Cilicia, I pray you may have good health in the Lord.
Machedonius bishop of Biritus, I pray you may have good health in the Lord.
Eusebius bishop of Dorilaium, I pray you may have good health in the Lord.
Basil bishop of Anquira, I pray you may have good health in the Lord.
Prohaeresius bishop of Sinopa, I pray you may have good health in the Lord.
Eustathius bishop of Epiphania, I pray you may have good health in the Lord.
Pancratius bishop of Parnasus, I pray you may have good health in the Lord.
Eusebius bishop of Pergamum, I pray you may have good health in the Lord.
Sabinianus bishop of Chadimena, I pray you may have good health in the Lord.
Bitinicus bishop of Zela, I pray you may have good health in the Lord.
Dominius bishop of Polidiane, I pray you may have good health in the Lord. /p. 76/
Pison bishop of Trocnada, I pray you may have good health in the Lord.
Cartherius bishop of Aspona, I pray you may have good health in the Lord.
Filetus bishop of Juliopolis, I pray you may have good health in the Lord.
Squirius bishop of Mareota, I pray you may have good health in the Lord.
Filetus bishop of Cratia, I pray you may have good health in the Lord.
Timasarcus bishop, I pray you may have good health in the Lord.
Eusebius bishop of Magnesia, I pray you may have good health in the Lord.
Quirius bishop of Filadelphia, I pray you may have good health in the Lord.
Pison bishop of Adana, I pray you may have good health in the Lord.
Thimotheus bishop, I pray you may have good health in the Lord.

Eudemon bishop of Thanis, I pray you may have good health in the Lord.

Callinicus bishop of Pelusium, I pray you may have good health in the Lord.

Eusebius, bishop of Pergamum, I pray you may have good health in the Lord.

Leucadas bishop of Ilium, I pray you may have good health in the Lord.

Niconius bishop of Troas, I pray you may have good health in the Lord.

Adamantius bishop of Cius, I pray you may have good health in the Lord.

Edesius bishop of Cous, I pray you may have good health in the Lord.

Theodulus bishop of Neocaesarea, I pray you may have good health in the Lord.

Sion bishop, I pray you may have good health in the Lord. /p. 77/

Theogenes bishop of Licia, I pray you may have good health in the Lord.

Florentius bishop of Ancyra, I pray you may have good health in the Lord.

Isaac bishop of Letus, I pray you may have good health in the Lord.

Eudemon bishop (I have subscribed for him), I pray you may have good health in the Lord.

Agapius bishop of Thenus, I pray you may have good health in the Lord.

Bassus bishop of Carpathus, I pray you may have good health in the Lord.

Narcissus of Irenopolis, I pray you may have good health in the Lord.

Ambracius bishop of Miletus, I pray you may have good health in the Lord.

Lucius bishop of Antinoüs, I pray you may have good health in the Lord.

Nonnius bishop of Laudocia, I pray you may have good health in the Lord.

Pantagatus bishop of Attalia, I pray you may have good health in the Lord.

Flaccus bishop of Ieropolis, I pray you may have good health in the Lord.

Sisinnius bishop of Perge, I pray you may have good health in the Lord.

Diogenes bishop, I pray you may have good health in the Lord.

Cresconius bishop, I pray you may have good health in the Lord.
Nestorius bishop, I pray you may have good health in the Lord.
Ammonius bishop, I pray you may have good health in the Lord.
Eugenius bishop, I pray you may have good health in the Lord. /p. 78/
Antonius bishop of Bosra, I pray you may have good health in the Lord.
Demofilus bishop of Beroe, I pray you may have good health in the Lord.
Euticius bishop of Filippopolis, I pray you may have good health in the Lord.
Severus bishop of Gabula, I pray you may have good health in the Lord.
Thimotheus bishop of Ancialus, I pray you may have good health in the Lord.
Valens bishop of Mursa, I pray you may have good health in the Lord.

Here ends the decree of the synod of Eastern bishops on the Arian side at Sardica, sent by them to Africa.

[III] /p. 103/ *Copy of the letter of the synod of Sardica to all the churches.*

1. Much and often have the Arian heretics ventured against God's servants who guard correct Catholic faith. /p. 104/ They have introduced, indeed, counterfeit teaching and have attempted to persecute the orthodox. So far have they rebelled now against the faith that it has not passed unnoticed by the religious devotion of the most clement Emperors. So, by the aid of divine grace, the most clement Emperors have gathered together a sacred council at Serdica drawn from various provinces and cities, and allowed it to take place, so that all disagreement might be removed, and, with false doctrine utterly rejected, only Christian religion be guarded by all. Bishops came from the East, /p. 105/ at the bidding of the most religious Emperors, principally because there was much talk about our very dear brothers and fellow bishops Athanasius, bishop of Alexandria, and Marcellus, bishop of Ancyro-Galatia. We think, indeed, that slanders against them have reached you too; and doubtless these people have tried to impress your ears to believe what they say against innocent men and to conceal suspicion of their own villainous heresy. But it was not granted them to

do this for long; for the governor of the churches is the Lord, who underwent death for the churches and for us all, and who, /p. 106/ for the sake of those churches has given us all a way up to heaven.

2. Eusebius, Maris, Theodore, Diognitus, Ursatius and Valens wrote to Julius our fellow priest and bishop of Rome some time ago, against the aforesaid fellow bishops Athanasius and Marcellus; bishops from other places also wrote, testifying to the innocence of Athanasius our fellow bishop and declaring Eusebius' account to be nothing but /p. 107/ a pack of lies. For although they refused the summons by bishop Julius, our very dear brother, the reason why they refused is apparent from the very letters whereby their lies are detected; for they would have come, had they had confidence in what they did against our fellow bishops, though their doings at this holy and great council have betrayed the design of their falsehood even more clearly: they came to Serdica and, on seeing Athanasius, Marcellus, Asclepius and the others, were afraid to come to judgement. /p. 108/ Though summoned not once or twice but frequently, they disregarded the invitation of the synod of all us bishops who had convened, and specially the aged Ossius, who, by virtue of age, confession and faith proven for such a long time and because of his having undertaken such labour for the Church's good, is accounted most worthy of all reverence. All were waiting for them and urging them to come to judgement, so that they could fully prove in person all that they had said or written about our fellow-ministers when these were absent. As we said before, though invited they did not come and thereby they demonstrated their own falsehood and only betrayed the fabricated trickery or studied cunning which they practised by their /p. 109/ refusal. For those who are confident of proving what they say when not present, are ready to demonstrate it in person. But because they dared not come, we consider that in future nobody should be ignorant of the fact that, although they may wish to practise their mischief again, they are quite incapable of proving anything against our fellow-ministers, whom they were accusing when these were absent but when they were present they fled them.

3. They fled, very dear brethren, not only because of those they falsely accused, but also because of those gathering from various places to convict them of many crimes. Returned exiles displayed their irons and

bands; and again /p. 110/ men still in exile sent associates and close relatives, friends and brothers, who reported the complaints of the survivors or followed up the undeserved wrong of those dead in exile. And, most importantly, there were bishops present, one of whom displayed the iron and chains he had worn on his neck through them, and others bore witness to death-threats arising from their false accusations. They had reached such a pitch of desperation that they would even have killed bishops, had these not escaped their blood-stained hands. Our fellow bishop, the blessed Theodulus, died whilst fleeing their attack; as a result of this false accusation his death had been ordered. /p. 111/ Others showed sword marks, blows and scars, others complained of having been tortured with hunger. And it was not people of no note who attested these things but it was picked men from all the churches, for the sake of which they had convened here, who were making known what had happened: the armed soldiers, the crowds with cudgels, the judges' menaces, the submission of false letters (false letters composed by Theognitus against our fellow bishops Athanasius and Marcellus, designed to move the Emperor against them, were read, and the proof of their falsehood was given by those who were Theognitus' deacons at the time) and besides these, the stripping of virgins, the burnings of churches and the imprisonment of God's ministers. All these things are due to the wicked and abominable heresy of the /p. 112/ Ario-maniacs. Those who refused communion with them had to endure the suffering of these things.

4. They took note, therefore, of this and saw they were in a critical position. They were ashamed to confess what they had done, since it was because they were no longer able to hide it any longer that they had come at last to Serdica in order, by their presence, to seem to rule out the suspicion that their acts were wrong. For seeing the victims of their false testimonies, and having as accusers from the other side those they had vehemently opposed, before their eyes, they betrayed the consciousness of their own crimes, and, though summoned /p. 113/ they would not come. Especially were they disturbed by their guilty awareness of our fellow-ministers Athanasius, Marcellus and Asclepius, who begged for justice and challenged their accusers not just to prove them guilty of what they had falsely fabricated against them but to inform them as to what the impious and wrongful acts they had

committed against the churches were. However, they were possessed of
such terror that they took to flight, and by this very flight uncovered
and exposed their own falsehood.

5.[1] Though their falsehood and wickedness is shown up not only from
the preceding events but from these as well, yet lest from this flight /p.
ll4/ they might be able to invent some excuse for other malpractice, we
thought what had done ought to be examined with truth and reason. We
found that they had been liars on these matters too and had simply made
an insidious attack upon our fellow-ministers. The man named Arsenius
they said Athanasius had killed is numbered among the living; and so
it was obvious from this that the rest of their vaunted claims were full
of lies and falsehood. Because they said certain things about a chalice's
having been broken by Macharius, Athanasius' presbyter, those present
from the same place in Alexandria testified that no such event ever
occurred there. Moreover, /p. 115/ bishops writing from Egypt to Julius
our fellow-minister amply affirmed that no suspicion of this sort was
entertained there. They say they have also records of proceedings
against him. But those they have are confessedly composed in the
absence of one party. Yet in these very records pagans and catechumens
were interrogated and one of the catechumens under interrogation said
he had been inside when Macharius made his entry; and another under
interrogation said this notorious Scyrus was lying sick in his cell. From
this it is plain that the sacrament could not have been celebrated at all,
since there were catechumens inside, and Scyrus was not inside /p. 116/
but lying sick. Scyrus himself, a contriver of all wickedness, said
Athanasius had burned a volume of the divine scriptures. When proved
false on this point he began to acknowledge that he had been sick when
Macharius was present, so that he showed from this too that he was a
false witness. Subsequently as a reward for his falsehood they gave this
same Scyrus the honour of the episcopate, a man who was not even a

---

[1]Para. 5: *Arsenius*] A Melitian bishop of Hypselis, and apparently an important figure in
the Church whose most prominent bishop was John Arcaph. For the story, exaggerated
by the Church historians, see Socrates' *History of the Church* [CPG 6028] I, 27 - 29,
Sozomen's *History of the Church* [CPG 2127] II, 23 - 25, Athanasius' *Defence against
the Arians 69*. The Easterns did not make any charge on this subject (cf. no. II, Para. 6).
ibid. *..catechumens...inside*] I.e. in the church amongst the baptized, whence they were
excluded for the eucharist.
ibid.: *Melitius*] See Introduction ii (b) p.xvii.

presbyter. Two presbyters came to the council who had at one time been with Melitius and having afterwards been received by Alexander, bishop of Alexandria, of blessed memory, now work with Athanasius. They testified that Scyrus had never been Melitius' presbyter nor had Melitius ever had in that very /p. 117/ place in the Mareotis either a church or a minister. Yet it is this man they have produced with them as a bishop, a man who was not even a presbyter, in order that they may seem to hide the falsehood from their hearers by the word 'bishop'.

6.[1] Moreover, the book, written by our brother and fellow-bishop Marcellus, was read, and the artful malice of Eusebius and his associates discovered. For they pretended that the propositions Marcellus set down for discussion were put forward by him as agreed and approved. There were read, therefore, the passages subsequent to and preceding the point at issue, and his true belief was discovered; for /p. 118/ he did not, as they falsely alleged, allocate God the Word a beginning from the holy Virgin Mary, nor did he write that his kingdom would have an end, but that it is without beginning and without end. Asclepius our fellow bishop brought forward the proceedings compiled at Antioch in the presence of the opponents and of Eusebius of Caesarea, and Marcellus demonstrated from the decisions of the episcopal judges that he was not guilty.

7. Though frequently called, they rightly dared not come and rightly defaulted, driven by the impulse of their own consciousness of guilt. By their default they corroborated their own falsehoods and gave credence to what their accusers, who were present, said and demonstrated. What else can we say? /p. 119/ Besides all this, they have not only received people long since deposed and flung out of the Church for the heresy of Arius, but have even promoted them to higher posts: deacons to the presbyterate, presbyters to the episcopate; for no other reason but to be able to promulgate more widely their irreligious doctrine and to corrupt true faith. The following are, after the two Eusebiuses, the current leaders of these people: Theodorus of Heraclia, Narcissus of Neronias in Cilicia, Stephen of Antioch, George of Laudocia (though he was

---

[1]Para. 6. ...at Antioch] In 341.

afraid to be present from the East), Acacius of Caesarea in Palestine, Menofantus of Ephesus in Asia, Ursacius of Singidunum in Maesia, Valens of Myrsa in Pannonia. Indeed, /p. 120/ the aforesaid bishops did not permit those who accompanied them from the East to enter the sacred council or to approach God's holy church at all. For on coming to Serdica they conducted assemblies amongst themselves at various places and threatened those coming to Serdica that they were not to go forward to the hearing at all or to unite in assembly with the holy synod. They came to the gathering only to make their presence known, and took to their heels at once. This, indeed, /p.121/ we have been able to ascertain from our fellow ministers, Arius of Palestine and Stephen of Arabia, who accompanied them but withdrew from their dishonesty. Arius and Stephen, on coming to the assembly, complained of the violence they had suffered, saying that nothing was done aright by those people and adding this: that many were there of sound faith whom they had prevented from coming by their threats against us. So, for that reason, they did their best to keep them all in one spot and did not allow them their freedom even briefly.

8.[1] Therefore, because it was our duty not to stay silent or leave unpunished /p. 122/ the falsehoods, the bonds, the murders, attacks, false letters, beatings, exposures of virgins, exiles, demolitions of churches, arsons, translations from small to larger churches and, above all, the teachings of the Arian heresy which attack orthodox belief: for that reason, we pronounce guiltless and innocent our very dear brothers and fellow-bishops Athanasius of Alexandria and Marcellus of Ancyra in Galatia, Asclepius of Gaza and their companions in ministry to God. And we are writing to each of the provinces to let the people of each church know the integrity of their bishop and that they do have a bishop of their own ; but as for those who /p.123/ have infiltrated their churches like wolves (i.e. Gregory in Alexandria, Basil in Ancyra and Quincianus in Gaza) the people are to know that these do not have the title of bishop and they are not to share in communion with them in any way or receive letters from any of them or write to them. But those i.e.

---

[1]**Para. 8**: *..Gregory...Basil in Ancyra*] Gregory was Athanasius' replacement, 338 - 345, Basil, Marcellus' at Ancyra. Basil was deposed, on grounds of violence towards the 'Anomeans', Aëtius and Eunomius, in 359 (see Introduction 2[b]).

Theodore, Narcissus, Acacius, Stephen, Ursatius and Valens, Menofantus and George (though George, as has been said was afraid to be present, but nevertheless because /p. 124/ he was thrown out by Alexander, of blessed memory, formerly bishop of Alexandria and because he is, just like the others included, of the Arian madness and because of the crimes laid to his charge) all of them, the holy synod has unanimously degraded from the episcopate, and we have judged not only that they are not to be bishops but that they are to have no communion with the faithful; for by separating the Son, and estranging the Word, from the Father, it behoves them to be separated from the Catholic Church and strangers to the name of 'Christian'. Let them, then, be anathema to us, inasmuch as they have dared to adulterate the word of truth [cf. 2 Cor 2:17; 4:2] whose apostolic ordinance is: 'If anyone preaches /p. 125/ to you things other than you have received, let him be anathema' [Gal 1:9]. We give order that none is to communicate with them, for there is no agreement between light and darkness [2 Cor 6:14]. Order them to keep afar, for there is no partnership of Christ and Belial [2 Cor 6:15]. Be on your guard, very dear brothers, neither to write to them nor to receive their letters. Take care, very dear brothers and fellow-ministers, as being yourselves present in spirit at this synod [1 Cor 5:3; col 2:5], to confirm by your own writings all that we have enacted, so that /p. 126/ from your written assent it may be manifest that all the bishops are of one mind and one will. We pray, brothers, for your good health in the Lord.

Here ends the letter.[1]

[IV] *A copy*[2] *of the letter written to Julius, bishop of Rome, and sent to bishop Julius by the synod.*

1. What we have ever believed is even now our mind; for experience tests and corroborates what anyone has heard with the ear. What the most blessed master of the gentiles, Paul the apostle. said of himself, is true: 'Though I am absent in the flesh I am with you in spirit' [Col

---

[1]Para. 8: *Here ends*] Excerptor's note.
[2]Heading: *A copy...*] Heading by the excerptor. The text, derived from Hilary's book, made its way into other collections.

2:5]. Because the Lord Christ dwelt in him, it is quite impossible to
doubt that the Spirit spoke through his soul and gave utterance through
the vehicle of his body [2 Cor 13:3]. So you too, very dear brother,
parted though you are in body, have been here in harmony with us in
mind and will [cf. 1 Cor 5:3; Col 2:5]. The reason for your absence was
the honourable and unavoidable fear that schismatic wolves might /p.
127/ steal and snatch away by craft or that heretical curs made mad by
savage rage might yelp or that the serpent, the Devil, might for sure
pour forth the poison of his blasphemies. For this will seem to be the
best and most fitting thing: if the Lord's bishops make reference to the
head, that is to the throne of Peter the apostle, concerning each and
every province.[1]

2. It seems almost superfluous, of course, to set down in this letter all
the events, proceedings and enactments, since they are contained in
written texts; and the living voices of our very dear brothers and fellow
presbyters Arcydamus and Filoxenus, and of our very dear son, the
deacon Leo, will have been able to set them out most truly and reliably.
It has been obvious to all how there have been assembled from the
Eastern regions those who call themselves bishops (though certain of
them are known to be leaders whose sacrilegious minds have been
tainted by the noisome poison of the Arian heresy) and that for a long
time they have been reluctant, owing to their lack of faith, to come to
a judicial hearing and have refused to do so, finding fault with
communion with you and us, a communion fully blameless since not
only did we believe the eighty bishops who each bore witness to
Athanasius' innocence, but they, on being convoked, by your presbyters
and your letter, to the synod which was due to take place /p. 128/ in
Rome, refused to attend; and it would have been quite unjust to refuse
Marcellus and Athanasius association, when these people spurned the
invitation and when so many bishops offered their testimony to
Marcellus and Athanasius.

---

[1] Para. 1: *if...province.*] It is *Western* bishops who use this respectful language which
articulates their general if not universal practice; the Easterns felt differently about the
(admittedly special) majesty of Rome.

3.[1] There were three things to be dealt with. The most religious
Emperors themselves gave leave for all points at issue to be discussed
afresh and, principally, the issues relating to the holy faith and
violations of the integrity of truth. Secondly, they gave leave that if
those who said that they had been ejected by an unfair judgement could
prove it, there should be a just confirmation of their status. The third
point at issue (and the one that may be called the true point at issue) is
that they had inflicted serious and grievous injuries, had heaped
insufferable and wrongful insults upon the churches, by seizing bishops,
presbyters, deacons and clergy generally, and exiling them, transporting
them to desert places, killing them with hunger, thirst, nakedness and all
manner of deprivation. Others they put in filthy stinking jails, several
they put in iron chains so that their necks were choked with the tight
collar bands. In the end, some of them, unjustly tortured by this same
confinement, expired, and nobody can doubt they died a glorious
martyrs' death. They still /p. 129/ dare to hold certain people whose
sole offence was to resist and exclaim that they abominated the Arian
and Eusebian heresy and refused to have communion with such people
and would not help those who preferred to serve the world. People
earlier thrown out have not only been taken back but even raised to
clerical office as a reward for their falsehood.

4.[2] But hear, most blessed brother, what has been decided about the
irreligious and immature young men Ursacius and Valens, since it was
plain that they do not cease spreading the deadly seeds of counterfeit
doctrine [Matt 13:24ff and parallels] and that Valens had left his church
intending to enter upon another. At the time when he instigated his
rebellion, one of our brothers, Viator, unable to take flight, was mobbed
and trampled upon in that very Aquileia, dying two days later. The
cause of his death was certainly Valens, who had induced the
disturbance. What /p.130/ we have notified to the most blessed Augusti,
will, when you read it, easily persuade you that we have omitted
nothing so far as was reasonable. And, not to make a long story tedious,
we have made known the acts they committed.

---

[1] Para. 3: ..*themselves gave leave*...] No imperial decree convening the Council and
defining its terms of reference ('pre-illuminating' it, was the later term), survives.
[2] Para. 4: *Viator*] Otherwise unknown.

5. Your excellent prudence should ensure by writing that our brothers in Sicily, Sardinia and Italy are acquainted with the proceedings and decisions, and do not in ignorance receive letters of communion from those deposed by a just sentence. But Marcellus, Athanasius and Asclepius are to continue in our communion, because no obstacle could be afforded by an unfair judgement and by the default and refusal of those who would not come to a court of all of us bishops who convened. As we mentioned above, a full report from the brothers your Charity sent here, will fully apprise your cordial self of the rest. We have been at pains to append the names of those dismissed for their misdemeanours, so that your exceedingly weighty person may know the identity of the excommunicates. As we said before, please see fit to warn all our brothers and fellow bishops not to accept letters of communion from them.

/p. 131/ The names of the heretics are:-
Ursacius of Singidunum
Valens of Mirsa
Narcissus of Irenopolis
Stephen of Antioch
Acacius of Caesarea
Menofantus of Efesus
George of Laudocia
The names of the bishops present at the synod and subscribing the judgement are:
/p. 132/ Ossius of Cordoba in Spain
Annianus of Castolona in Spain
Florentius of Emerita in Spain
Domitianus of Asturica in Spain
Castus of Caesarea Augusta in Spain
/p. 133/ Praetextatus of Barcilona in Spain
Maximus of Luca in Tuscia
Bassus of Dioclecianopolis in Machedonia
Porfirius of Filippi in Machedonia
Marcellus of Ancyra in Galatia
Euterius of Gannos in Thrace
Asclepius of Gaza in Palestine
Museus of Thebes in Tessaly

/p. 134/ Vincentius of Capua in Campania
Januarius of Beneventum in Campania
Protogenes of Serdica in Dacia
Dioscorus of Terasia
Himeneus of Ypata in Tessaly
Lucius of Cainopolis in Thrace
Lucius of Verona in Italy
Evagrius of Eraclia Linci in Machedonia
/p. 135/ Julius of Thebes Eptapilos in Acaia
Zosimus of Lignidus in Machedonia
Athenodorus of Elatea in Achaia
Diodorus of Tenedos in Asia
Alexander of Larissa in Thessaly
Aethius of Tessalonica in Macedonia
Vitalis of Aquae in Dacia Ripensis
/p. 136/ Paregorius of Scupi in Dardania
Trifon of Macaria in Acaia
Athanasius of Alexandria
Gaudentius of Naisus in Dacia
Jonas of Particopolis in Machedonia
Alypius of Megara in Acaia
Machedonius of Ulpiani in Dardania
/p.137/ Calvus of Castramartis in Dacia Ripensis
Fortunatianus of Aquileia in Italy
Plutarcus of Patras in Acaia
Eliodorus of Nicopolis
Euterius of the Pannonias
Arius of Palestine
Asterius of Arabia
Socras of Asofoebia in Acaia
Stercorius of Canusium in Apulia
/p. 138/ Calepodius of Neapolis in Campania
Ireneus of Scirus in Acaia
Martyrius of Naupactus in Acaia
Dionisius of Elida in Acaia
Severus of Ravenna in Italy
Ursacius of Brixa in Italy
Protasius of Milan in Italy

Marcus of Siscia in Savia
Verissimus of Lyons in Gaul
/p. 139/ Valens of Iscus in Dacia Ripensis
Palladius of Dium in Machedonia
Geroncius of Bereu in Machedonia
Alexander of Ciparissia in Acaia
Euticius of Motoni in Acaia
Alexander of Coroni in Acaia
59 bishops in total.

[V] /p. 140/ *(Narrative text)*

1. The matter needs, I think, no further explanation. Everything has
been published and portrayed in such a manner as to be brought out into
the light of knowledge. Bishops had been assembled from Egypt,
Athanasius was there in person. There was an indecent departure of
false judges at night, caused by their sense of guilt; there was the deep
odium, visible to all, attaching to such great misdeeds. Add to that the
initial grounds which served as a pretext for condemning Athanasius: he
was alleged to be responsible for the overturning of an altar, where
Scyras the presbyter was ministering, by the violent act of his presbyter
at the very hour of sacrifice. It is denied that Scyras is a presbyter and
the falsehood of the charge is condemned along with its author. But the
work of sacrifice cannot have taken place without a presbyter; and as
well as the man being at issue, there is no place even for so grave a
deed: there is no church in the Mareotis. Has the very religion of the
area become extinct, or is the place, where the sacrifice was profaned,
wont to sink into a chasm? Scyras, it is asserted, was ordained bishop
from the diaconate, in order that the authority of a lying bishop might
be superior to the constant abuse suffered in a presbyter. But if the
church had a location, it has it now; if not now, it did not have one.
And which is less credible: that these judges of falsified charges should
have suggested that what clearly did not take place did take place; or,
that those, who judged subsequently should have decided that something
which if it was cannot not have been, was not?

2. Therefore anybody trained by human habits to the use of our common intelligence, anybody embarking upon the path to truth and following the maxims of prudence, should take heed and consider what view he should hold in matters of this kind. Meanwhile I say no more of the authors of the judgements. These two decisions are to stand forth: one affirming a criminal act, naming the place /p.141/ and designating the injured man; the other, denying crime, place and man. I ask what decision you think it is just to concur with. It is certain, I think, that anybody asked for his opinion by each party and mediating between the two decisions will say: 'If there is an offence, it must be made known; if there is a place, it must be demonstrable; if there is a man, he must be observable'. But since there is no reliable evidence for the deed, the place has no religion and there is no injured party, it will be thought mad for a judge to decide over non-existent matters.

3.[1] Look at the sky and the stars, you bishops, and at him who made these from nothing [2 Macc 7:28], look with the freedom of the faith and hope you received [cf. Gal 5:13], remembering that this pattern of future judgement upon yourselves had been set out: 'With the judgement that you have been judged, will you be judged' [Matt 7:2]. Answer my question: 'By what judgement do you condemn Athanasius?' You say, of course: 'By the bishops' judgement' and this will be the excuse for your confession. 'We have followed a sacred regard for judgements subject to episcopal communion'. But will you deny that you have ignored the communion restored by Ossius, Maximinus and Julius to Athanasius whose condemnation Valens, Ursatius and Saturninus exacted from you? I do not make a comparison; I ask what your opinion was about Athanasius' offence. It is said that his presbyter, Macharius, rushed into the church in the Mareotis, interrupted Scyras the presbyter and overturned the sacraments of our salvation. Witnesses of the affair, a catechumen and a pagan, were cross-examined. But are you unaware that subsequently it was decided that there was no church in the Mareotis and that Scyras was not a presbyter? What *did* you follow?

---

[1] Para. 3: ..*you bishops*] Hilary addresses his contemporary audience: the bishops who *now* condemn Athanasius, pressurized by Valens and the rest.
ibid.: ' *'We have followed...communion* '] I.e. 'because we are a fellowship of bishops, we have respected their decisions'.

You grant authority to false bishops, deny it to true bishops. Realities you decree non-existent, but judge /p. 142/ the non-existent. My belief is that prison has forced you, the warder has made you, the torturer has pressed you, the sword has hung over you, the fire has burned you, to make you believe this allegation. Dishonesty acquired episcopal authority amongst you when non-existent events were judged, sacredness lost its trustworthiness when truth should have been maintained. The disciples of Christ! Worthy successors of Peter and Paul! Pious fathers of the Church! Pompous ambassadors between God and people, you have bartered Christ's truth for men's falsehood.

We have dealt enough with the first theme: our undertaking to show that Athanasius could not have been held responsible for any of the charges laid against him. It remains for me to speak very briefly of what happened over Marcellus and Fotinus.

4.[1] Fotinus, bishop of Sirmium, was trained by Marcellus; at one time he was a deacon under him. The habits and teachings of innocence were corrupted and he persisted in disturbing evangelical truth with novel preachings. And this so often, that as the increase of his faults produced a loss of love for God, so his mad zeal for depraved knowledge grew stronger. Accordingly, bishops gathered from a large number of provinces, to remove Fotinus, who had already been condemned as a heretic two years before at a synod at Milan, from the episcopate. The bishops were all the more anxious and wary of a repetition of the general trouble and confusion, because it had been necessary hitherto for a number of bishops responsible for false judgements against Athanasius or communion with the Arian heresy to be cut off from the Church. Ursacius and Valens took advantage of the opportunity to approach the bishop of Rome and begged to be received back into the Church, asking to be pardoned and admitted to communion. Julius, in his wisdom, granted the pardon they asked for, in order to drain strength from the

---

[1] Para. 4: *Fotinus...Marcellus*] How Fotinus' teaching developed out of Marcellus' is not clear. He is alleged to have taught that Christ was (nothing but) a human being. He probably said that Christ, as God's Logos, is Jesus i.e. that even 'Logos', which, Marcellus had taught, designated the pre-incarnate Word, meant only the son of Mary in his special role as revealer of God's mind. Something to the effect that a divine hypostasis ('subject'), if it descended from heaven, would have to leave its divinity behind, seems to have been a sally of his.

Arians for the gain of the Catholic Church, by admitting those who had grievously disturbed the unity, repentant (as they now were) of this plot and their foolhardiness, into Catholic communion through the granting of a peaceful reconciliation. And because there is no confession except of truth, no repentance except of a fault, no pardon except of a misdeed, Valens and Ursacius, on being admitted as they asked, /p. 143/ into communion, made a prior acknowledgement of Athanasius' innocence and of the falsehood of the judgement; and atoned for the Arianism in the following letter:-

[VI] *Copy[1] of the letter written at Rome in his own hand by Valens and signed by Ursacius, after the Easterns' declaration that Athanasius was not guilty.*

Valens and Ursacius to the blessed lord and pope Julius.

  Since it is agreed that hitherto we have made many grave allegations in our letters against the reputation of bishop Athanasius, and on being convened by the letters of your holiness have not presented any grounds for the matter we published, we declare to your holiness, in the presence of all our brother presbyters that all the reports about the reputation of the aforesaid Athanasius which have hitherto reached your ears, are /p. 144/ false allegations by us, lacking any validity; and therefore we most willingly embrace communion with the aforesaid Athanasius, especially since your holiness has seen fit to pardon our mistake in accordance with your natural generosity. We declare, too, that should the Easterns, or even Athanasius himself, wish, at any time, maliciously to summon us to a legal suit, we shall not be present without your knowledge and agreement. But as for the heretic Arius and his accomplices who say 'there was a time when the Son did not exist'; who say 'the Son is from nothing' and who deny that God's Son existed before the ages: we declare that both now and always we have anathematized them by this

---

[1] Heading: *Copy...*] Hilary's own note, apparently. A Greek translation of the document, by Paulinus of Trier, appears in Athanasius' *Defence against the Arians* 58 and *History of the Arians* [CPG 2127] 26; also (thence?) in Sozomen's *History of the Church* III, 24 and the medieval Nicephorus' *History of the Church* IX, 27. The document seems to have come to Hilary directly from the Roman archives: 'in his own hand'.
  ...was sent two years after...] to Julius presumably, in 347.

very hand with which we write, just as we did through our earlier
document which we presented at Milan. And we repeat what we said
above: that we have condemned in perpetuity the Arian heresy and its
instigators. *In Ursacius' hand:* I, Ursacius, bishop, have subscribed to
this declaration. /p. 145/

This letter was sent two years after the heresy of Fotinus was
condemned by the Romans.

[VII] *Copy[1] of a second letter from Valens and Ursacius, which they
sent to bishop Athanasius from Aquileia somewhat later than they sent
the above letter.*

Ursacius and Valens to our lord and brother Athanasius.
  Our brother Moyses' coming to your Charity, dear brother, has given
an opportunity for us to convey to you, through him, our warmest
greetings from Aquileia and our prayers that you may be in good health
when you read our letter. You will give us confidence, if you also
recompense us by writing back to us in return. You are, of course, to
know by this letter that we are at peace with you and have ecclesiastical
communion with you. May the divine kindness guard you, brother! /p.
146/

[VIII] (*Narrative text*)

1. On the writing of the above letters the petitioners were favoured with
a pardon and a return to the Catholic faith with communion was granted
them, especially in view of the fact that the petitioners' letters asking
for pardon maintained the truth of the synod of Serdica. Meanwhile
there was an assembly at Sirmium. Fotinus, apprehended as a heretic,
and a long time earlier pronounced guilty and for some time cut off
from united communion, could not even then be brought through a
popular faction ...

---

[1]No. VII, Heading: *Copy...*] As above, Hilary's own note apparently. Greek translation
also as noted before in no. VI.

But Athanasius himself excluded Marcellus from communion, who had been restored to the episcopate by the decision of the synod of Sardica, after a reading of the book he had written and published (we have a copy of it), when Marcellus saw fit to add in certain other novelties to hint vaguely at the path of doctrine on which Fotinus struck out. Athanasius did this prior to the censure of Fotinus, declaring the exercise of a corrupt will forestalled by the judgement and not condemning on the basis of the publication of the book. But because bad can easily be made out of good, he authorized not what had previously been done against Marcellus, but what was being done against Fotinus.

2.[1] This fact, however, ought to be known to all: no synod, apart from the one which was annulled by the decisions of Serdica, was ever thereafter got together against Marcellus; and when the Westerns gave their ruling on Fotinus and reported it to the Easterns no judgement was uttered against him. Cunning, ingenious, and persistently mischievous minds, though, sought an opportunity to reverse the judgement cancelled by Athanasius' acquittal, and, in writing back about Fotinus, they added a mention of Marcellus as the instigator of such teachings, in order that the novelty of the case might stir up into public recollection the issue of Athanasius, which was long since dead and buried by the judgement of truth; and might /p. 147/ surreptitiously use Fotinus' condemnation to attack Marcellus' reputation. In the text of the above letter it is obvious that Marcellus was condemned, along with Athanasius, by the Arians, on the pretext of the book Marcellus had published on the subjection of the Lord Christ. A reading of the book itself shows that an innocent man was seized upon. The reliable evidence of the still extant book proves the falsehood too of the Arian judgement. But, as custom required, letters were written to the Easterns about Fotinus merely by way of affording general knowledge and not, as now happened, of extorting agreement by an injustice.

---

[1] Para. 2: ..*in writing back about Fotinus*...] I.e. in response to the Council of Milan's condemnation of Fotinus.
ibid.: *above letter*] Absent through the lacuna.
ibid.: *This fact*....[Para. 3] *pressure from the synod*] Cf. Sulpicius Severus *Chronicle* [CPL 474] II, 37.

3.[1] But why was it reported that Athanasius was responsible for the refusal of communion to Marcellus? Was Marcellus kept back on account of the defects in the book? They are themselves witnesses to Fotinus' having taken the starting point for his perverse teaching from Marcellus' lessons. For when Athanasius declined communion with him, Marcellus kept back from entering the Church. Communion entered upon with him means belief in Christ's subjection and the surrender of his kingdom; declined, on the other hand, it shows the perversity of either teaching. And thus both decisions of this man are without fault, since in the gift of communion he followed the mind of the synod, but in the refusal of communion he is without fault, because Marcellus himself made the renunciation on his own without any pressure from the synod. But this whole issue of either cause is also one of sorrow. And although amends were made for the hatred of him so long harboured against Athanasius, nevertheless so great an endeavour proceded to a higher stage of wickedness.

4.[2] For I have a third topic. Let me point out the creed the letters established at the outset. It is fraudulent, heretical, and though its words are beguiling I will show it to be full of poison within. For we declare: that there is one unbegotten God the Father, and his one unique Son, God from God, light from light, first-born of all creation; and we add as third the Holy Ghost the Paraclete. And so, when unsuspecting readers or simple untutored souls /p. 148/ have been taken in by such soothing beginnings, they pass over from the common and unified assent

---

[1] Para. 3: ..*reported...Marcellus?*] The whole paragraph is hard to understand: partly because we do not have the Easterns' letter; partly because Hilary has an awkward point to explain viz. Athanasius' ambiguous relationship with Marcellus. I think it means: Why did the Easterns write back that Athanasius had condemned Marcellus because he was no longer in communion with him? (Athanasius never condemned Marcellus, though he acknowledged he had 'had a case to answer' - see Epiphanius' story about Athanasius, who smiled broadly as he made the admission, *Panarion* [CPG 3745] 72.4.4). Hilary's answer is that the two were not in communion with each other but without condemnation on Athanasius' part of Marcellus' published views.
ibid.: ...*entering the Church.*] i.e. communicating in the sacraments with Catholic christians.
ibid.: ..*mind of the synod*] i.e. of Milan.
ibid.:But this whole issue...sorrow] cf. Phoebadius of Agen *Against the Arians* [CPL 473] 8.
[2] Para. 4: ..*established at the outset.*] i.e. and set down at the beginning, presumably of their letter.

of the subscription elicited in censure of Fotinus, to Athanasius' guilt and the condemnation of the Catholic faith. And I hope that the synod of Serdica will have furnished no small portion of understanding of this fact, for here all the charges against Athanasius are shown to have been concocted by Arian hostility and violence was done to God's people, so that they might pass on to a pestilential connivance with their deadly doctrine. However, let me briefly state the whole matter, because the case demands it.

5.[1] It has always been the duty and function of apostolic men, by continual public proclamation of the faith in its completeness, to suppress the attempted yelps of heresy and, by setting forth the truth of the gospels, to extinguish the frowardness of erroneous doctrine, lest it infect the minds of hearers with some spot and pollute them with the contagion of the blemish accompanying it. And so they often and at length summed up with loving care in various epistles what ought to be our thought of God the Father, our knowledge of God the Son and our hallowing in the Holy Ghost, in order that God the Son might be known to be from God the Father, God the Father to be in God the Son and God the Son in God the Father. And thus, according to his own formulation: 'The Father and I are one' [Jn 10:30] and, again, 'Just as, Father, you in me and I in you' [Jn 17:21]; our faith in God is contained in the names and persons of Father and Son. Indeed, there are no other grounds for our envy by the Jews, hatred by the pagans and mad rage by the heretics than our professing in the Father the eternity, power and name of the Son. The stubborn wrongness of heretics /p. 149/ has always originated from their irreligious belief. Preoccupied in bad ways, their backs turned on harmless tasks, they involve themselves in profitless and difficult questions; rendered objectionable by their lives, their inclination, their cast of mind, they endeavour to please by the novelty of their teaching after they have lost the knowledge of the truth.

---

[1] Para. 5: ..*lest it infect...accompanying it*: Cf. Gregory of Elvira *On the faith* [CPL 551] 3.
ibid.: ..*our faith...and Son*] Cf. Gregory ibid., 7.

6.[1] When therefore it had become known to our fathers that the two Ariuses had arisen, preachers of a most irreligious creed, and it was no longer a conjecture about this blot, but a considered view of it that had become widely spread, they sped from all parts of the earth to converge upon Nicea; in order that the faith might be presented to lay people, the path of divine knowledge made straight in the light of understanding, and the seedbed of the emerging evil killed off within their propagators. The Ariuses taught the following sorts of thing: 'God the Father begat the Son to create the world and in accordance with his own power made him into a new substance, a second substance and a second new God'. It was profanation of the Father to suppose anything like him could be generated from nothing; it was blasphemy against Christ to despoil him of the inherited excellence of his Father's boundlessness. The result was that though they had been taught by the Father's spokesman: 'There is no other God but me' [Is 45:18]; and by the Son: 'I am in the Father and the Father in me' [Jn 14:11] and 'The Father and I are one' [Jn 10:30], they broke the link of sacred unity in the two belonging to the substance not existing by creation, awarding God's Son, our Lord Jesus Christ, temporal beginning, origination from nothing, secondary name.

7.[2] To suppress this evil, 300 or more bishops assembled at Nicea. By the assent of all, a condemnation for heresy was pronounced against all Arians; /p. 150/ the teachings of the gospels and the apostles were unfolded and the perfect light of Catholic unity was raised aloft. What, therefore, was made explicit, the creed itself, as published, entrusts to us.

---

[1] Para. 6: *two Ariuses*] There was another Arius involved with the presbyter of Baucalis and 'heresiarch', but probably Hilary means Eusebius of Nicomedia+Arius or the two Eusebiuses.
ibid.: *When therefore...second new God*] Cf. Sulpicius Severus *Chronicle* [CPL 474] II, 35.
ibid.: *They sped...Nicea*] Cf. Phoebadius *Against the Arians* 6.
ibid.: *God the Father... world'*] Cf.ibid. 22.
[2] Para. 7: *To suppress...Arians*] Cf. Phoebadius op. cit., 6.

[IX] *The Creed[1] written at Nicea by 318 bishops against all heresies.*

We believe in one God, the Father Almighty, maker of things visible and invisible.

And in one Lord Jesus Christ, the Son of God, born of the Father, that is from the Father's substance, God from God, light from light, true God from true God, born not made, of one substance with the Father (what the Greeks call *omousion*) and through him were made all things whether in heaven or on earth; who, for us men and for our salvation, came down, was incarnate, made man, suffered and rose again on the third day, ascended into heaven and will come again to judge quick and dead.

And in the Holy Ghost.

But as for those who say 'there was when he was not' and 'before he was born, he was not' and that 'he was made from non-existents' (what the Greeks call *ex uc onton*) 'or from a different substance' calling God's Son 'mutable and changeable': these the Catholic and Apostolic Church anathematizes. /p. 151/

(Narrative Text)

1.[2] A comparison of the creeds discloses the falsehood of the design. The creed laid down at Nicea is full and perfect and, with all the points where heretics are wont to creep in barred, is knit together with the solidarity of the everlasting union between Father and Son; whereas the other soothes by its simplicity in first declaring we believe as, God forbid anybody should believe. The creed of the Westerns, however, founded in the teachings of the gospels acknowledges the Father in the Son and the Son in the Father; the Father unbegotten, the Son eternal with the substance of eternity i.e. as the Father is ever, so also is the

---

[1] No. IX *The creed...*] Excerptor's note. For an account of the text of the creed, see G.L. Dossetti *Il Simbolo di Nicea e di Constantinopoli* (Rome. 1967).

[2] Para. 1:..*with all...Father and Son*] Cf. Gregory of Elvira op. cit., 1. Para. 1: *The creed of the Westerns...of whom he is*] Cf. ibid., 3.

Son ever in the Father and is God born of God without conception, i.e. is ever in him of whom he is.

2.[1] But this profession of, not faith but, faithlessness, says 'God from God', gives us 'first-born' and teaches the name of the Trinity. It covers up its poison under the unassuming guise of religious modesty, saying 'God from God, 'light from light'. It takes advantage of this declaration to teach that he exists as God and light, 'made' by God from God and light and not as 'begotten' from God i.e. not from the substance of the Father's eternity; and thus to ensure that by insulting the Father the Son is cheapened, if he is a God originated from nothing. They intend by 'first-born' to designate a certain order for the creation of the realities of the world beginning from his origination; and so, because time is involved in the world's existence, Christ's existence, though prior to the world, will be involved in time, and there will be no pre-temporal eternity in him. So created things will have order in time, and, through his being before it, it will follow that he began to exist in time /p. 152/ and all that is God in Christ will be nullified, since in him there will be a temporal origination from the once non-existent Mary.

3.[2] Not but what men, void of all good hope claim apostolic authority as a pretext for such a dangerous idea, because he is called 'first-born of every creature' [Col 1:15]. However it is by leaving out the preceding and following sentences that they manufacture a suitable handle for their own teachings. This is the sequence of statements: 'Who is the image of the invisible God, first-born of all creation, because in him are constituted all things in heaven and on earth, visible and invisible, whether thrones or dominations, principalities or powers; all things were established through him and in him, and he is before all' [Col 1:15-17]. 'The image', then, 'of the invisible God', I am to believe, exists and begins in time. Or it is that because he is 'the first-born of all creation', a certain order of creating is manifested which is

[1] Para. 2: *But this ...faithlessness*] Cf. Phoebadius op.cit., 3. ibid.:
It covers...from nothing] Cf. Gregory of Elvira op. cit., 3.
ibid.: *It covers...modesty*] Cf. ibid., 1.
ibid.: *They intend...origination*] Cf. ibid., 2.
ibid.: *..and all...Mary*] Cf. Phoebadius op. cit., 9.
[2] Para. 3: *..because in him there already ..create*] Cf. ibid., 21.

knit together and produced together, in him? But does not, 'because in him are constituted all things in heaven and on earth' follow 'first-born of all creation': meaning that the material of all the universe's elements, visible and invisible, is founded and constituted in him and that therefore 'all things are through him and in him'? Therefore he is the 'first-born of all creation' because in him there already existed from the beginning all the origins of all the generations he was going to create. In this way he is not numerically first in a series of creatures arranged in order, but remaining 'image of the invisible God' by the power, ever in him, to create, he will have maintained himself 'first-born' of those things which were created through him in heaven and on earth, the visible and invisible existents. /p. 153/

4. There is, to be sure, a not dissimilar weaving together of falsehoods in the naming of the Trinity. For as soon as they have impiously and scurrilously severed Son from Father in diverse substances, and creative power is present in the separated two, a third is counted in the Spirit; and so, though the Father is in the Son and the Son in the Father, and though the Holy Ghost receives from both inasmuch as the Spirit is declared the inviolable unity of this Holy Trinity, the Trinity as spoken of by the heretical party gives birth to division.

5.[1] But the careful treatment of the Nicene creed, and its language complete, as it is, in the strictest teaching of truth, have put an end to the ingenious devices of heretics by the proposition: 'We believe in one God the Father and in his one Son Jesus Christ'. Both together and both separately, are 'one': 'one' in the personal name of 'Father' and in that of 'Son'; 'one', because both constitute one God. 'True God from true God' teaches the worth and appellation common to both in equal truth, and that different conceptions are not involved; since each is 'one', God from God and true from true. But since 'one' exists in each, 'born not made' refers to the property originating by birth, because to be made implies 'out of nothing' whereas to be born from the Father is peculiar to him, and those that are born have no other pattern or worth than that

---

[1] Para. 5: *..since each...from true*] Cf. Gregory of Elvira op. cit., 7.
ibid. : *For 'being'...its eternity*] Cf. Phoebadius op. cit., 7.
ibid.: . *...so that...eternity*] Cf. Gregory of Elvira op.cit., 8.

of their origin. But what is made exists as a result of an action to make it be. And in him the making does not begin from nothing, but he has been born from the parent. 'Of one substance with the Father' (what the Greeks call *omousion*) means this: only eternity is like itself, and, because ever in being, in God. Therefore, lest the Lord Jesus Christ should be tarnished by the stain of wicked heresy, in him therefore is unfolded the truth of being. For 'being' takes its name from that which ever is. Since it /p. 154/ never needs external aid for its self-maintenance, it is also called 'substance', because it is internally that which ever is and subsists in the worth of its eternity. And thus, because he says 'The Father and I are one' [Jn 10:30]; and 'He who has seen me has seen the Father' [Jn 14:9]; 'I am in the Father and the Father in me' [Jn 14:10] and 'I came forth from the Father' [Jn 16:28.]; one and the same substance of eternity equal in both finds its completion in both, i.e. in the God who is ingenerate and in the God who is begotten.

The phrases 'came down', 'was incarnate, 'was made man' and 'rose again on the third day and will come again to judge quick and dead' contain the mysteries of our salvation. Therefore he is 'immutable' and 'unchangeable' Son of God, so that, in the assumption of man, he brought glory upon corruption rather than tarnish upon eternity. By the anathema against those who say 'he was made from nothing' (what the Greeks call *ex uc onton*) and against those who say 'there was when he was not' and 'before he was born he was not', they mark them out under a curse, and assign damnation in Christ for the profanation of his eternity, that is the Godhead he inherited from his Father.

6. Athanasius, deacon at the synod of Nicea and subsequently bishop of Alexandria, had stood forth, therefore, as the forceful instigator of this creed's publication to all. Holding fast to truth he had vanquished the Arian plague in the whole of Egypt and when witnesses conspired against him on that account, a false set of charges was prepared. The affair was afterwards decided by the reliable decisions of the judges. But it will assist understanding, if the address of the council of Sardica to Constantius, after Athanasius' acquittal, be taken note of.

[X] /p. 181/ *Address of the Synod of Sardica to the Emperor Constantius.*[1]

1. Your kindly nature, most blessed lord Augustus, unites with a kind will, and since mercy flows forth in abundance from the fount of the sense of religion you inherit, we are sure of obtaining readily what we ask. Not only with words, but also with tears, we beseech you that Catholic churches be no longer afflicted with most grave wrongs, no longer undergo persecutions and insults even (which is abominable!) from our brethren. Let your clemency take thought and decree that all judges everywhere, who are entrusted with the direction of provinces and to whom ought to belong only the care and concern for public business, should refrain from attention to religion, should not hereafter take upon themselves functions not rightly theirs and expect to investigate the suits of the /p. 182/ clergy, or to vex and harry innocent men with various pains, with threats, violence and terror.

2. Your unique and wonderful wisdom understands that the unwilling and reluctant should not, and ought not, to be driven or compelled to submit or yield under duress to those who are ceaseless in scattering the corrupt seeds of counterfeit doctrine. For that reason you govern the state by elaborate and wholesome plans, you keep watch and are on your guard to see that all whom you rule possess sweet liberty. In no other way could troubles be quieted, divisions mended, save by each one's having full power to live unconstricted by the exigency of a state of bondage. Yes, your Gentleness ought to listen to the cry of those who say: 'I am Catholic, I will not be a heretic; I am Christian not Arian; and it would be better for me to die in this age than to ruin the virgin chastity of truth through the overweening power of some private person'. And, most glorious Augustus, it should seem just to your Sanctity, that those who fear the Lord God and divine judgement, should not be tainted or defiled by abominable blasphemies but should have the power to follow those bishops and leaders who preserve inviolate the covenants of love and who desire to have lasting and genuine peace. It cannot be, nor will reason suffer it, that contraries

---

[1] No. X, Heading: Excerptor's note.

should agree, things dissimilar cohere, false and true be merged, light and darkness be confounded, day and night have any association [cf. 2 Cor 6:14]. If, therefore, as we have no hesitation in hoping and believing, these things move that kindness of yours which is not instilled but innate, /p. 183/ give order that governors show no attentiveness, no favour or partiality of situations to grave heretics. Let your Gentleness allow congregations to hear teaching them those they have willed, those they have deemed fit, those they have chosen. Let them celebrate together the solemnities of the divine mysteries, and offer prayers for your safety and happiness.

3.[1] Let no froward or envious person utter ill-willed words! Let there be no hint even of rebellion or troublesome murmuring! Let all things be silent and respectful. As it is, those who are sullied by the infection of the Arian disease, do not cease ruining the genuineness of the gospels with their impious tongues and sacrilegious minds and perverting the right rule of the Apostles. The divine prophets they do not understand. Cunning and astute, they make use of an artifice to veil the deadly corruption within of their carefully contrived words, so that they do not emit their poisonous power before they capture and ensnare simple innocent souls under cover of the name of 'Christian' (lest they alone should perish) but make them guilty partners in their own horrible offence.

4. This too we beg your Piety: order those still detained in exile or deserted places (distinguished bishops, indeed, remarkable for their worthiness of so great a title) to return to their sees, so everywhere there may be pleasing liberty and joyful happiness.

5. Who does not see, who does not understand? After nearly 400 years since the Only-begotten Son of God /p. 184/ saw fit to come to the aid of a perishing humanity, and as if there had been no apostles in earlier days, nor after the martyrdoms and deaths of these, any Christians, there is now shed abroad not a novel and most loathsome plague of foul atmosphere but the Arian plague of abominable blasphemies. Did those

---

[1] Para. 3: *The divine prophets...offence*] Cf. Phoebadius op. cit., 15.

who believed in earlier days have a vain hope of immortality? We have
been informed that these falsehoods have recently been invented by the
two Eusebiuses, by Narcissus, Theodore, Stephen, Acacius, Menofantus
and by Ursacius and Valens, two young men, ignorant and headstrong.
Their letters are published and those who listen to them yapping rather
than arguing, are even convinced by suitable 'evidences'. Those who
unwisely and incautiously hold communion with them, by becoming
associates in their misdeeds, will of necessity share their crimes, and,
being cast out and disinherited in this age will suffer eternal
punishments when the day of judgement comes.

[XI] (*Narrative Text*)

1. Nobody will be in any doubt that these holy men took such trouble
over Athanasius' acquittal that after the Synod's decisions, which right
required the priestly (the churchly) conscience to maintain out of due
regard to the priestly judgement, it behoved them to write to the
sovereign and draw up a delegation. But what else /p. 185/ do they beg
for in this letter but freedom for the faith from the contagion of the
name of Arius? What else do they ask for but that chains, imprisonment,
tribunals, all that funereal condition, and even fresh investigations of
those responsible, be checked? God has taught, rather than compelled,
the knowledge of himself and acquires authority for his ordinances by
awe at the operations of things heavenly, disdaining the
acknowledgement of a coerced will. Had force of that kind been applied
in regard to the true faith, the teaching of the bishops would have
encountered it and said: 'The Lord is God of the universe; he has no
need of compelled compliance, he does not ask for a coerced
acknowledgement. He is not to be beguiled but conciliated, not
reverenced for his sake, but for ours. I can receive only the willing, hear
only the praying, note only the professing. In simpleness he is to be
sought, in acknowledgement he is to be learned, in love he is to be
delighted in, in uprightness of will he is to be kept hold of.' But what
is this? Priests are compelled by chains, ordered by punishments, to fear
God. Priests are held in jails, lay-people are set in the tight confinement
of a series of chains, virgins are stripped as a punishment and bodies
consecrated to God are exposed to public gaze, fitted out as fodder for

the shows and the inquisition. They compel people, into the bargain, to become, all of them, not Christians but Arians. They wickedly wrest a faith professed in God into a fellowship with their guilt. Sanctioning these things, even, by the authority of their own name they lead an upright Emperor into error, and so give themselves, under the guise of the fear of God, subjects in this perversity. They demand inquisitions, they require the aid of judges, they /p. 186/ beg for royal authority. Nor even so do they blush at the perversity of their wrong-doing: at their having been unable to extort the connivance of the common people even by right of compulsion.

2.[1] Had these things been presented from ancient documents and brought to the notice of our present era, there would, I believe, have been doubt about such extraordinary things. Moreover when a demand was made that all the others should pronounce a man guilty, there would have been an inquiry into the reliability of the documents, into the lives of the judges, the credibility of the accusers, into the behaviour and actions of the man himself. For the united condemnation of the Arians would have put in motion his acquittal, and it would at once have been highly risky to nullify the decision without taking up again the inquiry into guilt and innocence; and all the authority of antiquity, along with the doctrine of faith, would have been available to itself in its own defence. But when those then condemned as Arian heretics, shake the empire, disturb everything and ruin all men, from power and ambition, and Athanasius too, if he was guilty can still be guilty; let the witnesses speak, let the judges see! Let the teaching of the faith shine forth from the instructions of the gospels and apostles! What a belabouring of the understanding there is! What a dullness of heart! What a forgetting of hope! What a love of wrong-doings! What a hatred of truth! They change the love of God into partiality for the damned.

---

[1] Para. 2: *But when...heretics*] Cf. Gregory of Elvira op. cit., 4.
ibid.: *What a belabouring...truth*] Cf. Phoebadius op. cit., 16.

3.[1] I come now to a recent event, in which even the acknowledgement of a wrong-doing disdained to keep itself from hiding its artifice. Bishop Eusebius of Vercelli is a man who has served God all his life. This /p. 187/ Eusebius, after the synod of Arles when bishop Paulinus had opposed their great misdeeds, was commanded to go to Milan. A synagogue of ill-willed people congregated there and for ten days he was forbidden to approach the church, whilst headstrong malice exhausted itself in opposition to so holy a man. Then, with all wise counsels put to sleep, it was seen fit that he be summoned. He was present along with the Roman clergy and bishop Lucifer of Sardinia. Brought to subscribe against Athanasius, he said: there ought first to be agreement on the reliability of the bishops, certain of those present had been found by him to be stained with heresy. He produced the Nicene creed, quoted above, promising to do all they demanded, if they wrote down the profession of faith. Dionisius of Milan was the first to accept the document. When he began to write down what was to be professed, Valens roughly wrenched pen and paper from his hands, crying out that no business could happen from then on. After much clamour the common people became aware of the matter. Great indignation arose in all. The creed was attacked by the bishops. So, out of healthy respect for the judgement of the populace, they crossed from the church to the palace. The decision speaks for itself as to the kind of decision they wrote at length against Eusebius, before they entered the church.........

---

[1] Para. 3: *Eusebius*] Much of what is important about him is revealed in our text: that he stuck firmly to his principles, despite pressure from Constantius who backed the Easterns in their demand for condemnation of Fotinus, Marcellus and Athanasius, and recognition of George as legitimate bishop of Alexandria. For discussion of his dignifed correspondence with Constantius, and for the significance of it for interpreting the evidence about the Edict of Arles (353) and Milan (355) see Smulders' Excursus II. (There is an English translation of Constantius' letter to him in P.R.Coleman-Norton's *Roman State and Christian Church* (London, 1966) no. 93). *Lucifer*, bishop c.350 - c. 370, left a literary legacy, much of it highly vituperative and a train of disasters for the Church of Antioch where he inaugurated a new succession of bishops.
ibid.: *Bishop Eusebius... entered the church*] Cf. Sulpicius Severus op. cit., II, 39.

HILARY OF POITIERS *AGAINST VALENS AND URSACIUS*

Book II

[I] /p. 155/ *A copy[1] of the letter of Liberius bishop of Rome to the Eastern bishops.*

 To our very dear brethren and all our fellow-bishops established throughout the East, I, Liberius bishop of Rome, send greeting of eternal salvation.

Eager for the peace and unanimity of the churches after I had received your Charities' letter about Athanasius and the rest addressed to bishop Julius of blessed memory, I followed the tradition of my predecessors and sent Lucius, Paul and Helianus, presbyters of Rome on my staff, to the aforesaid Athanasius in Alexandria, asking that he come to Rome so that the matter arising from ecclesiastical discipline in regard to him might be decided upon in his presence. I sent Athanasius a letter, through the aforesaid presbyters, in which it was stated that if he did not come, he was to know that he was a stranger to communion with the church of Rome. The presbyters returned with the message that he refused to come. Consequently, I have followed your Charities' letter, which you have sent us about the reputation of the aforesaid Athanasius, and you are to know by this letter I have sent to your united selves, that I am at peace with all of you and with all the bishops of the Catholic Church, but that the aforesaid Athanasius is estranged from my communion and that of the church of Rome and from association in Church letters.

---

[1] No. I, Heading: *A copy...*] Excerptor's heading. Probably this, together with the other letters of Liberius, came to Hilary from the Roman archives.
ibid.: *..letter ...memory*] The letter comes from a synod at Antioch in 352, which had deposed Athanasius and elected George (of Cappadocia) to replace him.

[II]¹ (*Narrative Text*)

Is there anything not holy in this letter, is there anything not issuing from the fear of God? But Potamius and Epictetus, whilst they rejoiced at the condemnation of the bishop of Rome, just as was concluded at the synod of Rimini, /p. 156/ refused to listen to these things. Indeed bishop Fortunatianus even sent the very same letter again to various bishops, without success. But the result was that he was more of a burden to himself in the denial of communion to Athanasius and made the whole affair risky for himself so long as he detracted nothing from the synod of Sardica because Athanasius had been acquitted and the Arians condemned, and letters sent from the whole of Egypt and Alexandria were giving warning that the same sort of letter as had been written a long time before to Julius about restoring communion to Athanasius in exile were now sent (as will be perceived from the subjoined) to Liberius about observing communion with him.

[III] /p. 89/ *The letter of the delegates, which was sent, through bishop Lucifer, to the Emperor Constantius, by Liberius bishop of Rome.*

Bishop Liberius to the most glorious Constantius Augustus.

1.² Most serene Emperor, I beg that your Clemency may give a kindly hearing to me, so that the theme of my thought can become evident to your gentle self. I am entitled to obtain this very thing without delay from a Christian emperor, son to Constantine of holy memory; yet therein I understand myself to be in a difficulty, because I cannot, by repeated amends bring your mind to reconcile itself with me, a mind forgiving even towards the guilty. For by your Piety's utterance, sent some time ago to the people, I am much wounded, I indeed, who must needs bear all things patiently; yet it is a marvel to me that your mind, which always has room for mildness, which never (as Scripture has it) retains its wrath till sunset [cf. Eph 4:26], holds fast its displeasure with

---

¹ No. II..*condemnation of...*] I.e. of Athanasius, *by* Liberius.
No. III,Heading: *Lucifer...*] The letter survives independently of Hilary amongst the letters of Lucifer. The heading is the excerptor's.

² Para. 1: *..utterance...people...*] Constantius had evidently complained about the intransigeance of Rome (as he saw it).

me. For, most religious Emperor, I seek true peace with you, a peace not built by words with an inner arrangement of guile, but one made strong with solid grounding in the teachings of the gospels. Not only the affair of Athanasius, but many other matters have become public, and because of these /p. 90/ I had besought your Gentleness that a council might be brought about, so that when (what your mind's unfeigned devotion to God particularly desires before all things!) the issue of faith, wherein resides foremost our hope in God, had been treated of, an end could be put to the affairs of those who ought to be in wonder at our concern for God. It was worthy of a worshipper of God, worthy of your empire which is ruled, and grows by, loyalty to Christ, that here particularly you should show clemency to us in obtaining these requests, out of your respect for the holy religion you care for with eagerness.

2.[1] Many are in haste to wound the members of the Church. They have concocted the charge that I held back letters in order that the crimes of a man, whom they were said to have condemned, should not become generally known: the letters from the Eastern bishops and the Egyptians, all of which contained the same charges against Athanasius. But it is quite clear to all, and nobody denies it, that we published the Easterns' letters, read them to the church, read them to the council and gave that answer to the Easterns too. We have not given our faith to the Easterns or decided in their favour, because at that very time the decision of 80 Egyptian bishops on Athanasius was contrary to theirs: a decision which we likewise rehearsed and intimated to the Italian bishops. And so it seemed to be against divine law, when the majority of bishops stood for Athanasius, to grant any degree of approval. Eusebius, who was their emissary, left us these documents, as he owes faith to God, on his speedy journey to Africa. However, all the subsequent documents have been conveyed by Vincentius, who was despatched along with the rest, to Arles, in case they might be insufficient to obtain a council.

3. Your wisdom, therefore, will see that nothing has entered my mind which it was unworthy of God's servants to think. /p. 91/ God is my witness, the whole Church along with its members is witness, that, just

---

[1] Para. 2: ..*their emissary*...] I.e. of the 80 Egyptian bishops.

as the reasoning of the gospels and apostles teaches, I, in the faith and fear of God, do spurn and have spurned all that is worldly. Living as a churchman, I have, not by mad boldness but by established and respected divine law and in the service of others, accomplished nothing pertaining to the law for the sake of bragging, nothing through lust for glory. To this office, as God is my witness, I came unwillingly. In it I desire to continue, so long as I am in this world, without offence to God. It has never been my own laws but those of the apostles that I have worked to make permanently assured and safeguarded. Following the practice and rule of my predecessors, I have added nothing to the office of the bishop of Rome, in nothing have I allowed it to be lessened. Preserving the faith which had taken its course through a succession of such great bishops, a greater part of whom were martyrs, I fervently wish that it may ever be kept unimpaired.

4.[1] Finally, care for the Church and duty itself persuade me to open a subject to your Piety. The Easterns notify me of their wish to be united with us in peace. What is peace, most clement Emperor, when there are, from those quarters, four bishops (Demofilus, Macedonius, Eudoxius and Martyrius) who eight years ago, after refusing at Milan to condemn the heretical views of Arius, walked out of the council in a rage? Your fairness and clemency will be able to judge whether it is right to assent to their opinions, whatever they may be or whatever risk they may have. It is no novelty that they now attest them in detail and under the pretext of Athanasius' reputation. Letters by the former bishop Alexander, addressed to Silvester of holy memory, are extant, and in these he gave notice prior to Athanasius' ordination /p. 92/ that he had expelled from the Church for following Arius' heresy, eleven men, presbyters as well as deacons. Certain of these are now said to occupy positions outside the Church and to have acquired little meeting-places; it is also affirmed that George in Alexandria communicates with them by letter. So what

---

[1] Para. 4: *Letters...extant...*]. These letters are only known of here, Sylvester was bishop 314 to 335.
ibid.,*George*] 'Intruder' in Alexandria 352 - 362. Elected, he could not enter into office and only did so in 357 when Athanasius had been forcibly removed. He was lynched by a mob angry at his assault upon sacred buildings of the old religion. The Emperor Julian protested (faintly) and asked for his library. The story is told in Socrates *History of the Church* III, 2f.

peace can there be, most serene Emperor, if, as has now happened throughout Italy, bishops are obliged to be obedient to the declared opinions of such people?

5. There is another point you should take into account, because your Serenity is patient and will allow of it. On hand are recently arrived letters of legates who had been despatched to your Clemency. In these they make known their previous intention of surrendering to the views of the Easterns, but that they had put forward a condition: if the same people condemned the heresy of Arius, they would be swayed by this example and would obey their views. As they themselves make plain, the matter was agreed. The Bible was sworn by. A council was entered into. A discussion was held and with it they had an answer that they could not condemn Arius' teaching, because their sole demand was that Athanasius should be deprived of communion. Hence your Clemency should consider this question too: ought the issue of the man to be carefully examined and dealt with, the rights of the Catholic religion having been correctly observed?

6. For this reason we should ask over and over again that in your gentleness and devotion of mind to God, you should have before your eyes, for the sake of the excellence of him who has proved to all mortal men how great he is in your defence, the kindnesses of him who rules your empire in all things and should diligently cause these matters to be treated of with all deliberation in an assembly of bishops, so that by God's grace the times may be rendered peaceful through you, and that with your Serenity's /p. 93/ consent all things may be discussed in such wise that what stands ratified by the judgement of God's priests (that all universally agreed on the exposition of faith ratified between such great bishops at the council of Nicea in the presence of your father of sacred memory) can be guarded with the precedent for the future, so that the Saviour himself, who surveys from aloft the intent of your mind, may rejoice at your having rightly put the issue of faith and peace before even the needs of the state by such great despatch of affairs. It seemed good that my brother and fellow bishop Lucifer, along with Pancracius the presbyter and the deacon Hilary, should set out to ask your Gentleness to deign to listen to our pleadings with a well-disposed mind. We trust it will not be hard for them to obtain from your Clemency,

with a view to the peace of all the catholic churches, a council. May the clemency of God almighty keep you safe for us, most clement and most religious Augustus.
Here it ends.[1]

[IV][2] /p.164/ Liberius, however, before going into exile, wrote this letter cast in the same form to the confessors in exile i.e. Eusebius, Dionisius, and Lucifer.

1. Although under the guise of peace the enemy of the human race seems to have waxed more savage in his attacks upon the members of the Church, /p. 165/ your extraordinary and unique faith has even here shown you, you priests most welcome to God, to be approved by God and has marked you out already for future glory as martyrs. So, placed as I am betwixt sorrow for your absence and joy at your glory, I am utterly unable to find the herald's tones of exultant praise in which I may proclaim the merits of your courage; save that I know that here I have set forth consolations more acceptable to you, if you may believe me thrust down in exile at the same time as you. Next, I am saddened enough that a harsher necessity meanwhile drags me from your company as I continue to hang in this state of waiting. For I desired, most devoted brethren, to be spent before you and on behalf of you all, so that your love might the more through me follow the pattern of glory. This, though, will be the prize for your merits: that as a result of the perseverance of your faith you come first to the brilliant glory of confession. I therefore ask your loving selves to believe me present with you and so to think me not absent in feeling, and to understand that I have pain enough in separation meanwhile from your company. In a word, the more you follow after glory, the more it can teach you that any who have been given their crowns in persecution could feel only a persecutor's murderous sword, whereas you, utterly devoted soldiers of God as you are, have had experience of false, hostile brothers, and have won a victory over men of perfidy. The more their violence could grow

---

[1] Para. 6: *Here it ends*] Scribe's or excerptor's note.
[2] No. IV, Heading: *Eusebius*] Three other letters from Liberius to him survive [CPL 1628].

in the world, the more /p. 166/ are they found bestowing the rewards of praise on priests. Thus you are to be sure of the heavenly promise.

2. And because you have been brought closer to God, lift me up, your fellow-minister and servant of God, by your prayers, to the Lord, that I may be able to bear with the added assaults which daily, as they are announced, inflict more grievous wounds, so that, with the faith unharmed and the position of the Catholic Church safe, the Lord may see fit to make me your peer. Because I long to have more reliable knowledge of what took place at the conference, I ask your holinesses to see fit to tell me all by letter, so that my mind, tortured by various rumours and my body's by now enfeebled powers, may be able to feel an added gain. /*And in another hand*/ May God keep you safe and sound, my lords and brothers.

[V] Moreover, Liberius, before going into exile, wrote about Vincentius of Capua to Caecilian, bishop of Spoleto, as follows:
I do not wish Vincentius' action to call you away from attending to a good deed, very dear brother.

[VI] /p.167/ He says the following to Ossius about Vincentius' collapse:-
Meanwhile (because I ought to omit nothing you do not know) many fellow- bishops from Italy assembled. They and I had begged the most religious Emperor Constantius to order, as it had pleased him to do some time before, the gathering of a council at Aquileia. I am letting your holiness know that Vincentius of Capua along with bishop Marcellus, likewise from Campania, undertook to be our legates. Because I had high hopes of him, since he maintained the cause very well and had often remained as judge in the same cause with your holiness, I had believed that the law of the gospels or of the legateship could be preserved intact. Not only did he obtain nothing, but he too was led into that deceit. After his action I was affected by a double grief and resolved that I had better die for God, lest I seem to be the latest traitor or to be concurring with opinions contrary to the gospel.

[VII] After all these things which Liberius had either done or promised to do, /p. 168/ he rendered all null and void after being exiled by writing to the Arian and heretical sham accusers who had wrongfully brought about the judgement against Athanasius the orthodox bishop:-

Greetings from Liberius to his very dear brothers, the Eastern presbyters and fellow bishops.

1.[1] Your holy faith is known to God and to men of good will for its godly fear. Inasmuch as the law says: 'Judge just things, sons of men' [Ps 58(57):1(2)], I did not defend Athanasius. But because bishop Julius, of good memory, my predecessor, had taken him up, I was afraid that I might perhaps be thought guilty of some prevarication. But, when I got to know in God's good time that you had condemned him justly, I thereupon concurred with your decisions. I have written an additional letter, to be conveyed by our brother Fortunatianus to the Emperor Constantius, likewise dealing with his reputation i.e. his condemnation. And so with the removal of Athanasius from communion /p. 169/ with us all, his letters are not received by me//*variant reading* : in addition to which the decisions of you all are received by me along with the apostolic see/ /I say that I am at peace with you all and in peace and harmony with all the Eastern bishops or, rather, throughout all the provinces.

2.[2] That you may know more truly that I express my true belief in this letter, let me say: because my lord and common brother Demofilus kindly saw fit to set forth your creed, which is also the Catholic faith, as discussed and set forth by the majority of our brothers and fellow bishops at Syrmium and accepted/†*this is Arian falsehood. By this sign I, not the apostate Liberius, have marked what follows*/by all present, I have accepted it gladly/†*Saint Hilary anathematizes him*: † *I*

---

[1] No. VII, Para. 1: *..in addition..by me*] The extra clause is printed by Feder in the apparatus. It occurs in manuscripts deriving from Hilary's text, but is not in manuscript A. It makes slightly odd syntax, but may well be genuine.

[2] Para. 2: *...creed...*] Probably the 'blasphemy' of Sirmium, set out in A. Hahn *Bibliothek der Symbole* (Breslau, 1897) no. 161. It rejected the use of *usia* and of the terms *homoüson* and *homoüsion* (= similar in substance). The matter has been the subject of much dispute; see Brennecke pp. 265ff, Hanson pp. 357ff.

anathematize you, Liberius, and your associates/. I have not contradicted
it in any respect, I have concurred with it, follow it and hold to it.
/Anathema to you, prevaricating Liberius, twice and thrice/. However,
I believe your holinesses, in view of the fact that you see me in entire
agreement with you, ought to be asked to see fit to work out in a joint
effort of planning, to what extent /p. 170/ I may be released from exile
and return to the see divinely entrusted to me.

[VIII][1] *(Narrative Text)*

These are the signatories to the false creed, written at Syrmium,
Liberius calls 'catholic' and says was set forth to him by Demofilus:-
Narcissus, Theodorus, Basil, Eudoxius, Demofilus, Cecropius, Silvanus,
Ursacius, Valens, Evagrius, Hireneus, Exuperantius, Terentianus, Bassus,
Gaudentius, Macedonius, Marcus, Acacius, Julius, Surinus, Simplicius
and Junior */All had to be heretics/.*

[IX][2] *From Liberius in exile to Ursacius, Valens and Germinius.*

1. Because I know you to be sons of peace, lovers of concord and
harmony in the Catholic Church, I address you, very dear lords and
brothers, by this letter. I have not been forced by any necessity, as God
is my witness, but do it for the good of the peace and concord which
has prior place to martyrdom. Your wise selves are to know that
Athanasius, who was the bishop of Alexandria, was condemned by me,
before /p. 171/ I wrote to the court of the holy Emperor, in accordance
with the letter of the Eastern bishops, that he was separated from
communion with the church of Rome; as the whole body of presbyters

---

[1] No. VIII: ... *false creed...set forth*] This is no. 160 in Hahn *op. cit.*,, 'False' it may be,
'Arian' in a strong sense it is not: Basil of Ancyra could sign it. If *this* is the only
Sirmium creed Liberius signed (see no. VII), his 'lapse' and 'betrayal' could be regarded
as (comparatively) light: he has not signed the 'blasphemy of Sirmium'. The natural
reading of nos. VII and VII is to identify what Liberius signed. But that is (probably)
wrong. He (probably) signed both: it was assent to the 'blasphemy' which alone could
procure his return to a see now troubled by an 'intruder' (Felix).
ibid.: *All... heretics.*] Another indignant scribal comment or the excerptor's note.
[2] No IX. Heading] By the excerptor.

of the church of Rome is witness. The sole reason for my appearing slower in writing letters about his reputation to our Eastern brothers and fellow-bishops, was in order that my legates, whom I had sent from Rome to the Court, or the bishops who had been deported, might both together, if possible, be recalled from exile.

2. But I want you to know this also: I asked my brother Fortunatianus to take to the most clement Emperor my letter to the Eastern bishops, in order that they too might know that I was separated from communion with Athanasius along with them. I believe his Piety will receive that letter with pleasure for the good of peace, and a copy of it I have also sent to the Emperor's trusty eunuch Hilary. Your Charities will perceive that I have done these things in a spirit of friendship and integrity. Which is why I address you in this letter and adjure you by God almighty and his Son Jesus Christ our Lord and God, to see fit to travel to the most clement Emperor Constantius /p. 172/ Augustus and ask him to order my return to the church divinely entrusted to me, for the sake of the peace and concord in which his Piety ever rejoices, in order that the church of Rome may undergo no distress in his days. But you ought by this letter of mine to know, very dear brothers, that I am at peace with you in a spirit of calm and honesty. Great will be the comfort you secure on the day of retribution, if through you has been restored the peace of the Roman church. I want our brothers and fellow bishops Epictetus and Auxentius also, to learn through you that I am at peace, and have ecclesastical communion, with them. I think they will be pleased to receive this news. But anyone who dissents from our peace and concord which, God willing, has been established throughout the world, is to know that he is separated from our communion /I say anathema to the prevaricator and the Arians/

[X] *From Liberius in exile to Vincentius.*

1. I do not inform you but recall to your mind, very dear brother, the fact that 'evil communications corrupt good manners' [1 Cor 15:33].

The wiles of evil men are well known to you, and through them I have
arrived at this distress. Pray that the Lord may grant /p. 173/ endurance.
My very beloved son, Urbicus the deacon, whom I seemed to have as
a comfort, has been taken away from me by Venerius the commissioner.

2. I believe it is being notified to your holiness that I have withdrawn
from that controversy over Athanasius' reputation and have written
letters to our Eastern brothers and fellow-bishops about him. Therefore,
because, God willing, we have peace everywhere, you will be seeing fit
to address all the bishops of Campania and let them know these things.
Write from them collectively, along with your letter about our
unanimity and peace, to the most clement Emperor, so that I too may
be able to be freed by him from misery. /And in his own hand/ My God
keep you safe and sound, brother. /A page written out in his own hand/
We are at peace with all the Eastern bishops and with you. I have
cleared myself with God, you will have seen. If you intend me to expire
in exile, God will judge between you and me [1 Sam 24:15 (16)].

[XI][1] /p. 93/ *A copy of the Emperor Constantius' letter to the Italian
bishops assembled at the Council of Rimini.*

The victorious Constantius Maximus the triumphant ever Augustus, to
the bishops.

1. Earlier statutes, reverend sirs, maintain that the sanctity of the law
relies upon matters ecclesiastical. We have ascertained sufficiently, and
more than sufficiently, from letters sent to our prudent self, that it is a
duty to attend to these same matters. Though assuredly that is
appropriate to the role of the bishops and /p. 94/ on this basis the well-
being of all peoples far and wide is made strong. But the present state
has urged a revival of ordinances. For no one will consider the
repetition of statutes unnecessary, since frequent reminders usually
increase attentiveness. These things being so, your Sincerities are to
recognize the need for a discussion on faith and unity and for attention

---

[1] No. XI, Heading: By the excerptor.

to be given to the provision of due order in matters ecclesiastical. For the prosperity of all peoples everywhere will extend and sure concord be secured, when your Sincerities have set in motion the consequences attendant upon the utter removal of all disputes on such things.

2.[1] This business should not overstrain your minds; for it would be improper for any decision to be made in your council about the Eastern bishops. Consequently you will have to deal only with those matters which your weighty selves recognize as pertinent to you, and on the speedy completion of the entirety should agree on the despatch of ten to my court, as we have given your prudent selves to understand in earlier letters. For the above-mentioned will be able to answer or discuss all the Easterns' proposals to them about the faith, so that a due end may be made of every issue and doubt laid to rest. These things being so, you should make no decree contrary to the Easterns. Indeed, if you mean to make any ruling contrary to them when the above-mentioned are not present, the product of a misused opportunity will be null and void and disappear. For no ruling attested by our ordinances as already now denied strength and validity could have any force. This being the case, you ought, sirs revered as governors of religion, to reach conclusions commanding respect and appropriate to presiding bishops, so that the demands of religion may be set out and none take advantage of what it is improper to venture upon. May the Godhead keep you safe for many a year, fathers. *Here it ends. Issued V Kal.Jun. in the consulship of Eusebius and Ypatius.*

[XII][2] /p.95/ *The definition maintained by all the Catholic bishops, before they were frightened by earthly power into associating with heretics, at the Council of Rimini.*

Thus we believe it can be agreed by all Catholics that we ought not to abandon the accepted creed whose soundness all of us in conference

---

[1] Para. 2: *Here it ends...Ypatius*] As the original document ended.

[2] No. XII, Heading: *The definition...Rimini*] Hilary's or the excerptor's heading. The beginning of a slightly different text of this document is also extant in a seventh century manuscript.

recognized, nor ought we to abandon the faith we received through the prophets from God the Father, through our Lord Jesus Christ by the teaching of the Holy Ghost and in all the gospels and apostles, and through the tradition of the fathers in succession from the apostles up to the proceedings at Nicea in opposition to the heresy which had arisen at that time: the faith which has established itself and continues to this present. To all these things we believe nothing can be added and from them /p. 96/ it is clear nothing can be taken away. It is agreed, therefore, that 'substance', both the term and the reality, is no novelty (a word intimated to our minds by many holy scriptures), and that it ought to maintain its established place. This reality and its name the Catholic Church with its godly doctrine has always agreed to acknowledge and profess.

[XIII][1] *(Narrative Text)*
All the Catholics with one accord subscribed to this definition. At the same council too, after it had been decided that the tradition of the fathers should not be lessened in any respect, all opponents of the tradition were condemned by the inspired voice of all with one accord. The following is a copy of the proceedings:-
Consulship of Eusebius and Ypatius, XII Kal. Aug.

When the synod of bishops had been gathered at Rimini and the faith had been under discussion, and minds had been settled as to the proper course of action, Graecianus, bishop of Calle, said: 'Very dear brothers, the Catholic synod has been as patient as decency allowed, and /p. 97/ has so often shown itself loyal to Ursacius and Valens, Germinius and Gaius, who by changing what they believed on so many occasions have thrown all the churches into confusion and are now attempting to introduce their own heretical thought into Christian minds. They want to overturn the consultation held at Nicea and set up in opposition to the Arian and all other heresies. Moreover, they brought us a creed they had written which it would have been wrong for us to accept. We pronounced them heretics a long time ago, and many days have made

---

[1] No XIII:*Very dear brothers...everlasting peace.*] Greek translation of this passage in Athanasius' *On the synods* 11.

good the judgement. We have not admitted them to our communion, condemning them in their own presence by our voice. Repeat now your decision, so that it may be confirmed by individual subscriptions'. All the bishops said: 'It is agreed that the above-named heretics be condemned, so that the Church, with the faith unshaken which is truly Catholic, may be able to abide in everlasting peace'. *Here it ends.*[1]

[XIV]² /p.78/ *The synod of Rimini to the most blessed and glorious Augustus Constantius*

1. At the bidding of God and by your Piety's command we believe it has been brought about that the bishops came from various provinces in the West to Rimini, so that the faith might become clear to all /p. 79/ Catholic churches and heretics be known. For when all we men of sound sense deliberated, we agreed that we should hold the faith which has endured from antiquity, was preached by prophets, gospels and apostles through God himself and our Lord Jesus Christ, saviour of your empire and bestower of your salvation, the faith which we have ever maintained. For we thought it wrong to mutilate any ordinance of those who sat together with /p. 80/ Constantine, your Piety's father, of glorious memory, in the proceedings at Nicea. That text was published and made known to the minds of ordinary people and from then on has been found a fixed barrier to the Arian heresy. Indeed not only the Arian, but all the other heresies, have been destroyed by it. If anything is taken from it, then a way will be thrown open for the poisons of heretics.

2. So, Ursacius and Valens came under suspicion of the same Arian heresy and were suspended from communion. They asked for pardon, as it says in their letters, and they had obtained it at that time from the council of Milan /p. 81/ with the assistance even of the legates of the Roman church. At Nicea, in Constantine's presence, a text was written

---

[1]*Here it ends*] Scribe's or excerptor's note.
² No XIV, Salutation: *The synod...Constantius*] Greek version of the letter in Athanasius' *On the synods* 10, Socrates' *History of the Church* II, 37, Sozomen's *History of the Church* IV, 18, Theodoret's *History of the Church* II, 19.

down with great care and Constantine held to it when he was baptized and departed to God's peace. We think it wrong, therefore, to mutilate it in any way or in any way set aside so many saints, confessors and successors to martyrs who were joint writers of the text, since, they preserved all that belonged to Catholics in the past in accordance with the scriptures. Their faith has lasted to the day your Piety received from God the Father through our Lord Jesus Christ the power to rule the world. But wretched, pitiable men have again boldly announced themselves as heralds of the impious doctrine and have /p. 82/ been attempting from that time on to pluck up what reason has planted. And when your Piety's letter commanded a discussion of the faith, we were offered, for our consideration, by the aforesaid disturbers of churches, in company with Germinius and Gaius, a sort of novelty containing many points of wrongheaded teaching. But when what they offered publicly in the council was seen to be out of favour, they thought it ought to be composed in a different way. Indeed it is obvious they have often altered these things in a short time. To avoid churches being disturbed too often, it was decided that the old decisions should be preserved assured and immutable. For the /p. 83/ information of your Clemency, therefore, we have sent legates to declare to you, by our letters, the council's view. The sole mandate we have given them is to carry through the legateship in such wise that the old decisions remain in the strongest force, and your Wisdom may know that peace cannot be effected on the assurance of the aforesaid Valens, Ursacius, Germinius and Gaius, were anything right taken away. Rather, indeed, a disturbance of all the regions and of the Roman church would be unleashed.

3. For this reason we ask your Clemency to hear with calm ears and look with a serene countenance upon all our legates and not allow any radical change detrimental to the old decisions, but to leave standing what we received from our forebears who, we are confident, were wise men and not in want of God's Holy Spirit, because by this /p. 84/ innovation not only are faithful laity being disturbed but the unbelieving are prevented from coming to faith. We pray too, that you will give orders that so many bishops who are in detention at Rimini (and, amongst them, very many afflicted with age and penury) should go back to their provinces, so that the lay-people of the churches may not be in difficulties, left on their own without bishops. This too is our repeated request: that there be no innovation, no lessening, but that there remain unharmed what has continued in the days of your sacred Piety's father and in your own religious era. Let not your Wisdom suffer us to be wearied or uprooted from our sees, but permit the bishops to be at rest with their people, free always to attend upon the prayers /p. 85/ they ever make for your salvation, for your kingdom and for that peace of yours which may the Godhead bestow on you, a peace deep and everlasting.

Our legates will carry the subscriptions and names of the bishops or legates, inasmuch as another document informs your holy and religious Wisdom of the same thing.

[XV] (*Narrative Text*)

The Catholic bishops subscribing to the pure creed sent ten legates with this letter to the Emperor. The heretical party notwithstanding, also sent ten legates from their body. When these latter reached the Emperor they were received, with the result that the legates of the Catholics were not received. These, wearied by a long delay and scared by the Emperor's menaces, condemned the pure creed which they had previously defended and accepted the false faith they had earlier condemned. You will find this to be the case from the following: *Here begin the proceedings at the point the episcopal legates turned aside from the true faith.*[1]

[XVI] In the consulship of Eusebius and Ypatius VI Id. Oct.

1. When the bishops /p. 86/ Restutus, Gregory, Honoratus, Arthemius, Yginus, Justin, Priscus, Primus, Taurinus, Lucius, Mustacius, Urbanus, Honoratus and Solutor had assembled in session in the province of Thrace at Nice at the posting place which had previously been called 'Ustodizo', Restutus, bishop of Carthage, said: 'Your wise selves know, most holy fellow-priests, that when discussion took place at Rimini on the faith, the argument created such a disagreement that there was, at the Devil's instigation, discord amongst God's priests. The upshot was that I, Restutus, and the group of bishops who followed us, gave sentence (I mean of segregation from our communion) against our brothers Ursacius, Valens, Germinius and Gaius as being the propounders of an evil view.

2. But because we have been in close touch with one another we have discussed everything and debated everything, and we have discovered what nobody can take offence at: that these men have in them by their own acknowledgement the catholic faith we have all subscribed to, and have never been heretics. So, because the harmony of peace is the most important thing with God, it is agreed that, by our common consent, everything dealt with at Rimini should be nullified, and that with God's favour complete communion with them should come about and nobody should remain in a disagreement which could or should sully them. And so, as I have said, because we are here present, each ought to say whether what I have followed is the right course, and subscribe with his own hand'. All the bishops said 'Yes' and subscribed.

---

[1] No XV:*Here begin...faith.*] Excerptor's heading.

[XVII]¹ *(Narrative Text)*

You will learn from the following what the confession of faith they subscribed, and Valens took with him to Rimini, was:- *Here it ends.* /p. 87/

[XVIII]² *Here begins a copy of the creed of the letter sent to the Emperor Constantius by the faithless bishops.*

To the deservedly most glorious lord and most victorious Augustus Constantius, from the synod of Rimini in concord with the Easterns (i.e. from Migdonius, Megasius, Valens, Epictetus and the rest of those in agreement with heresy).

1. Illumined by your Piety's writings we give and offer the greatest thanks to God because you have gladdened us by telling us what we ought to do in accordance with your Piety's discourse: nobody should ever use the words, unknown to God's Church, 'usia' or 'omousios', a usage which is wont to create a scandal amongst the brethren. We are most joyful that we have come to know again what we maintain. Blessed are we whom the so great good fortune has befallen that by your Piety's cognizance the rest, who are wont to apply these terms to God and God's Son, have accepted the due measure of defeat! We therefore render homage to your Clemency, because in our presence the essential marks of truth have shone forth, truth which knows no defeat and has won the victory; and so a term unworthy of God and never inscribed in holy laws, will now be used by nobody.

2. Because we are still being detained here where the synod took place and whence we sent a reply through our legates, we therefore ask your Piety to give orders that we, who hold on to pure teaching in agreement with the Easterns, may be dismissed and return to our people, so that from this side there may appear the lovers of truth who do not exchange

---

¹ No XVII:*Here it ends*] Scribe's or excerptor's note.
² No XVIII, Heading:*Here begins...bishops*] Excerptor's note.
i.e....heresy).] Hilary's note.

God for a term, and we, who hold catholic truth, may be no longer detained in company with people infected by perverse teaching. And so, sir, we earnestly entreat your Piety, before God the Father and the Lord Jesus Christ, God and God's Son, /p. 88/ make us, who have subscribed to healthy teaching and abandoned, at your command, the word 'usia', and order us to be be let go to our people, so that the Church, which absolutely refuses to change the words used of God and God's Son, may rejoice in the sovereignty of your power and glory, on which the Godhead has conferred so much that, with the coming to light of the sacrilege of the phraseology, the terms 'usia' and 'omousios', not found in the divine scriptures of God and God's Son, may depart.

3. Devout Emperor, aid the worshippers of God most high, aid those who pray to God the Father almighty through Christ, God's Son. Aid those who give a loyal hearing to your judgement, those who can worship none save God the Father through Our Lord Jesus Christ the Son of his glory [cf. Heb 1:3]. Command, lord Emperor, our return to our people by sending a letter to Taurus, prefect of the praetorian guard, because we render full obedience in our preaching of God's name to the Easterns and to your direction. Because we have always held firm in this affair, we ought now to go back to our people. We have sent letters about this affair to our Eastern fellow bishops, so that they may know we have always maintained this and continue in the Catholic faith with them. May divine piety make you ever most glorious and everywhere, in all things, vindicator, most devout lord Emperor *Here it ends.*[1]

[XIX][2] /p.174/ *Copy of the letter of the Eastern bishops, given to the legates returning from Rimini.*

Greetings in the Lord to the very beloved Ursatius, Valens, Magdonius, Megasius, Germinius, Gaius, Justin, Optatus, Marcialis and the rest of the synod of Rimini's legates; from Silvanus, Sofronius, Neo, Erodianus, Patritius, Helpidius, Theophilus, Theodorus, Eumatius,

---

[1] Para. 3: *Here it ends*] Excerptor's or scribe's note.
[2] No XIX, Heading: *Copy...Rimini*] Excerptor's or scribe's note

Didimion, Ecdicius, Arsenius, Passinicus, Valentinus, Eucarpius, Leontius, Eortasius and Macarius.

1.[1] We are eager for unity and peace, and, with a mandate from the synod to resist heresy, we have thought it right to make plain to you the circumstances affecting the Church, in case ignorance of them might make you associates of such great irreligion, although we do not suppose you to be unaware that we ourselves as the legates of the whole synod of a hundred and more bishops, have abstained with good cause up till now from entering this church. That is why we want you to be informed, so that the heresy now gaining mastery deep within the Church may not prevail. This heresy has dared to deny that Our Lord Jesus Christ the Only-begotten Son of God, God from God, is like the Father. We want you to be informed of this, so that you may have knowledge of the assertions and blasphemous statements about the Only-begotten God they are thinking and preaching. We have demonstrated this, indeed, to the most pious Emperor Constantius too, and he was moved with a most religious wish for the anathematization of all these things. However, a plot is now being hatched here: Aëtius, the author of this heresy, would be condemned rather than these irreligious utterances, so that sentence should appear to be given against the man rather than the doctrine. /p. 175/ We warn you, therefore, brothers, to re-examine these matters with care and to be at pains to ensure the continuance of the Catholic faith. But your Charities will be in no doubt that everything, as it occurs, is being told the Western churches. We wish you well, brothers, in the Lord.

---

[1] No XIX, Para. 1: *Aëtius*] For a short account, see best Hanson pp. 603 - 611. Born in the early 320s, died in Constantinople in the 360s, initially he lived mostly at Antioch where he enjoyed the confidence of its 'Arian' bishop, Leontius, and is said to have given instruction to (the future Emperor) Julian. Basil of Ancyra procured his banishment in 358 along with that of his more prominent pupil, Eunomius (in 360 made bishop of Cyzicus) on grounds of involvement with Gallus' conspiracy four years earlier. His theology irritated Constantius, who did not understand its denial of likeness in *substance* coupled with its assertion of exact likeness between Father and Son (see Introduction ii (b) p.xxi and was puzzled by the technical hermeneutics in general: story in Philostorgius' *History of the Church* [CPG 6032] IV, 12.

[XX]¹ *(Narrative Text)*

1. And so when this, to which the above mentioned blasphemies had
been annexed, had been received, a malicious charge was planned
against the one who had accepted it. Such a rage at the detection of
their false dealing had entered into them, that they put him in peril of
deposition. How painful it is to a guilty conscience that someone is
deterred by recognition of the truth! If this book of Valens and Ursacius
is not your creed, why do you not acquiesce in its condemnation? Is it
agreed amongst all, by the public assent of the human race, that poison
is bad, that the killing of an innocent person is a crime and that impiety
towards the Lord is a horrible thing? But anyone who does not condemn
these things when reported, must acknowledge himself an associate in
the practice of them; because there is no one who does not refute what
he hates and recommend what he has not refuted. For why is it that
when you came to Constantinople after the synod of Seleucia, you
joined immediately with the condemned heretics, did not postpone
somewhat the time of your arrival and did not, by reason of wise
counsel, bestow thought upon investigating the possibility of some delay
for yourselves? Next, there were present with you Eastern legates out
of communion with the bishops. They told you all that had happened.
They also pointed to heresy gaining the mastery. Ought you not at least
even now to have stood back and reserved yourselves as arbiters of all
the debates? But governed by awareness of some inclination or other of
your own, you did not accept the decision. You attached yourselves
immediately to your own people and /p. 176/ entered a partnership in
your blasphemies. Nor did you at the least take the advice that even if
some people had lost their sense of shame, the synod of Rimini counted.
For you betrayed your ruse immediately in not anathematizing your own
people.

2.² For in the midst of a large assembly of people asking you why you
did not call God's Son a creature, you answered that the holy people of
Rimini had not denied that Christ was a creature but one unlike the rest

¹ No.XX, Para 1: *..above mentioned...*] I.e. the creed of Nice.
² Para. 2: *..large assembly...*] At some public debate in Constantinople, where 'Anomean'
sympathizers were present to put the question.

of the creatures, because in the phrase 'he is not a creature like the rest of creatures' it had not been said that he was not a creation, but that he is not included with the rest; and so although he is utterly unlike the rest, nevertheless so as not to be another thing, but, as it were, another creature like the rest: in the way that an angel is like a man, or a man is like a bird or a bird like cattle. If these are my own lies, there are witnesses who were in the audience. But if they keep silent, your book you most impiously defended speaks with me, where it says Christ is as alien to God the Father as glass to a hyacinth. Next, has not your hypocrisy become plain, where you deceive listeners: because you also said 'he is not from non-existents but from God' since 'not from non-existents but from God' is in accordance with your profession, because the origin of anything's existence will be the same thing as the will that it should exist? I am obviously telling a lie if you condemned those who said he does not have his 'born-ness' by way of the substance but by way of the will, without the assistance of the Easterns through agreement with their own document. You profess him to be 'eternal' also 'with the Father'. Yes, you would have spoken aright, had my answer back not been: why did they proclaim that the true Only-begotten God was born of the true God the Father before eternal times, so that his eternity with the Father is the eternity of angels and human souls, not the eternity of things past but of things to come? You said also he is 'like, in accordance with the scriptures', as if, according to the scriptures, man is not like God [cf. Gen 1:26 etc] nor /p. 177/ a grain of mustard-seed [cf. Matt 15:31 and parallels], yeast [cf. Matt 13:33; Luke 13:21] or a net [Matt 13:47], like the kingdom of heaven. But it would be idle to run through your hypocritical falsehoods; your acts of impiety cry out against you.

3. A slave (I do not mean a good slave but a tolerable one) does not listen willingly to slander against his master, and avenges it, if he can; a soldier beats off danger to his king in submission of body and disregard of life. The dogs kept to guard a house understand by a natural sense and bark when they get the scent of people approaching them, and leap up all at once to confront the object of suspicion. You have heard it denied that Christ is God's Son and Only-begotten God. The imputation was being made that *you* deny it, and you kept quiet. Why do I speak of keeping quiet? You struggled against the protesters

and joined the clamourers. That was too little. Arms were taken up from your library to forward the preaching of impiety and with your assistance war against God began. Where, then, is your profession of faith at Nice in Thrace, in which you said all heresies were condemned? Your falsehood had been dragged forward into the light. The Sun of righteousness [Mal 4:2] has give over to his preachers the night of your profession of faith. For you approve these things and you condemn and you cross over to the heretics. Thus it is, that your very same previous deception practised to trick men, you have now employed to forward profession of avowed hatred of Christ our God.

HILARY OF POITIERS *AGAINST VALENS AND URSACIUS*

Book III

[I] /p.43/ *The Catholic[1] faith as expounded at Paris by the Gallican bishops to the Eastern bishops.*

Greetings from the Gallican bishops to all their most beloved and blessed Eastern fellow-bishops abiding in Christ throughout the various provinces.

1. With all consciousness of our life and faith we confess our thanks to God the Father through Our Lord Jesus Christ, because he has placed us in the light of the knowledge of his confession by the prophetic and apostolic teachings, so that we are not held fast in the judgement of this age by the shades of this age's ignorance, our sole and fullest hope of salvation being to confess God the Father Almighty through his Only-begotten Son the Lord Jesus Christ in the Holy Ghost. But certainly no less cause of our rejoicing is added daily, in that he frees us from the error of the world and does not suffer us to mix with the irredeemable fellowship of heretics. For we have learned, from your letter you entrusted to our beloved brother and fellow-priest Hilary, of the Devil's fraud and the heretics' minds conspiring against the Lord's Church, to deceive us by mutually divergent views, divided, as we are, in East and West. For the majority of those present at Rimini and Nice /p.44/ were forced on the authority of your name into silence on 'usia': a term you coined long ago against the Ario-maniacs and always taken by us in a holy and trustworthy way.

2. For we have embraced the term 'omousion' in reference to the true and genuine birth of the Only-begotten God from God the Father, detesting, as we do, that 'one' which accords with Sabellius' blasphemies. Nor do we understand the Son to be part of the Father, but to be whole and perfect Only-begotten God born from whole and perfect ingenerate God, and therefore confessed by us to be of one

---

[1] Heading: *The Catholic...bishops*] Excerptor's heading.

'usia' or 'substance' with the Father, lest he should seem a creature rather, or an adoption or an appellation, and because he is from him, as Son from Father, God from God, power from power, spirit from spirit, light from light; hearing, as we do, not unwillingly his likeness to God the Father (seeing he is 'the image of the invisible God' [Col 1:15]. But we mean only that likeness which befits the Father (that of true God to true God) in such wise that it is not the 'one' but the unity of the Godhead which is understood, because 'one' is single whereas unity is the plenitude of the born in accordance with the true reality of the birth, especially since the Lord Jesus Christ himself acknowledged to his disciples: 'The Father and I are one' [Jn 10:30]. By this not only does he signify his love for the Father but also the Godhead of God from God by the words: 'He who has seen me has also seen the Father' [Jn 14:9]; 'if you do not trust me, at any rate trust my works, because the Father is in me and I am in the Father' [Jn 10:38].

3. We hold this faith and shall hold it, abominating also those who say, 'He did not exist before he was born': not because we declare the Only-begotten God ingenerate, but because it is especially impious to make any time prior to the God of times, since that phrase 'before he was born he did not exist', is / p. 45/ temporal. Yet we do not deny that the Son is obedient to the Father even so far as death on a cross [cf. Phil 2:8], in accord with the weakness of the assumed man, since he himself said of his ascension to heaven: 'If you have loved me you will rejoice because I go to the Father, for the Father is greater than I' [Jn 14:28]. Through his assumption of flesh he deigned to name us his fellow brethren, since whilst remaining in the form of God he willed to be the form of a slave [cf. Phil 2:5ff].

4. And so, dearly beloved, since our simple selves recognize from your letter that in the silence on 'usia' we have experienced a painful deceit and since our brother Hilary, trusty preacher of the Lord's name, has given us the news that even their Pieties, who had returned from Rimini to Constantinople, were in agreement (as your accompanying letter testifies) and he could not move them to condemnation of such great blasphemies, we draw back from all the highly evil acts committed in ignorance. We have excommunicated Auxentius, Ursacius and Valens, Gaius, Megasius and Justin, in accordance with your letter and,

assuredly, as we said, in consequence of our brother Hilary's declaration who has refused to be at peace with those who have followed these people's errors. We also condemn all the blasphemies you have appended to your letter and specially we reject their apostate priests who have been put, either from ignorance or from impiety, into the positions of certain brothers most undeservedly in exile; and we promise and confess before God that anyone within Gaul who sees fit to oppose these decisions of ours is cast out of his chair of priesthood. Anybody, who without condemnation allows the opportunity of preaching otherwise, or who withstands God and Christ the Only-begotten God's majesty in some way other than we interpret from the meaning of 'omousion' /p.46/ will be judged unworthy of the sanctity of the name of bishop. By this your Charities are to know that Saturninus, who spoke most irreligiously against wholesome decrees, according to our brothers' two letters, has already been excommunicated by all the Gallican bishops. Old, though long hidden, crimes, and the proven irreligion of the novel audacity published in his letters have made him unworthy of the name of bishop.

Here ends the Catholic faith as expounded at Paris by the Gallican bishops to the Eastern bishops.

[II][1] Greetings in the Lord from bishop Eusebius to his lord and most holy bishop Gregory.

1.[2] I have received your Sincerity's letter, from which I have learned that, as befits a bishop and priest of God, you have withstood Ossius the transgressor, and, maintaining the creed written by the fathers at Nicea, you have refused assent to very many who fell at Rimini by their communicating with Valens, Ursacius and the rest whom they had

---

[1] No II, Salutation: *Gregory*] His floruit is c. 359 - c. 403. A writer of some distinction, his book *On the Faith* which draws upon Hilary, has a complex literary history but its first edition saw the light in 360 apparently (see Introduction iii [a]).

[2] Para. 1: *Ossius the transgressor*] He died in about 357 at a great age (he is reputed to have been a centenarian) after a lifetime of service, as the previous references to him in our text show: he presided over the Western bishops at Serdica and had held firm to the Nicene creed which he had been (partly) responsible for drawing up. Like Liberius he caved in, and at the end signed the 'Blasphemy' of Sirmium.

previously condemned on a recognized charge of blasphemy. We congratulate you for this, we congratulate ourselves too, that, in living in this resolve as you do and being strong in this faith, you have seen fit to remember us. But assure yourself (abiding, as you do, in this very confession and having no fellowship with the hypocrites) of our communion with you. With whatever treatises you can compose, with all the effort you can muster, reprove transgressors and chide the unfaithful, as you have done, undaunted by the kingdom of this present age, because he who is in us is greater than he who is in this world.

2.[1] /p.47/ But we, your fellow priests labouring in a third exile, say this which we think is plain: all the Ariomaniacs' hope hangs not on their disunited consensus but on the protection of the kingdom of this present age. They are ignorant of the words of scripture: 'Cursed are they who put their hope in man' [cf. 1 Jn 4:4]; 'but our help is in the name of the Lord, who made heaven and earth' [Jer 17:5]. We desire to endure in sufferings, so that (as it says) we can be made glorious in the kingdom [Ps 124 (123):8]. Please write to us and tell us your progress in correcting the wicked, and how many brothers you know are standing firm or have been set right by your admonition. All who are with me greet you, especially the deacons, and they all ask you, please, to greet with our respect all who stick loyally at your side. *Here ends the letter of Eusebius to Gregory the Spanish bishop* [cf. Rom 8:17].

[III][2] /p.156/ *A copy of the letter of Liberius, bishop of Rome sent to the Catholic bishops of Italy.*

Liberius,to the Catholic bishops throughout Italy who remain steadfast in the Lord, eternal salvation.

1. A return to his senses wipes out a man's fault of inexperience. Yet this we can see too from the holy scriptures: religion, we read, is beneficial for all things and is more important than bodily exercise

---

[1] Para. 2: *..third exile*] He was sent to Scythopolis, then to Cappadocia and finally the Thebaid, returning in 361.
ibid.: *all the Ariomaniacs...present age*] Cf. Eusebius of Vercelli *Letter to the presbyters and people of Italy[CPL 107]*.
[2] No III: Heading: *A copy...Italy*] Excerptor's note.

[1 Tim 4:8.], though that too has useful fruits. The condition of the present time demands that we follow religion. For nobody, if there is anybody, who deliberately aims at destruction by a harsher censure, is to consider this to be an innovation. Harshness is to be rejected, because protection is given /p.157/ from religion by apostolic authority, when it is said that there should be no sparing of those who acted in ignorance at Rimini, of those whose ignorance of wrong was a falling into the grip of error. I myself, indeed, have thought it best to weigh all these things with due measure, especially since both the Egyptians and the Achaeans had received people back, adopting the view that those, whom we have discussed above, should be spared, but the instigators condemned who have vexed innocent minds with the crooked and mischievous subtlety of the obscurity they have used to veil the truth, claiming darkness as light and light darkness [cf. Is 5:20].

2.[1] Therefore, anybody who returns to his senses and recognizes the grip of ignorance by the very gentle assistance of our words, after having experienced in himself that poisonous, cunning and hidden plague of Arian dogma, is to be restored by draining it out, by condemning its instigators passionately and vehemently, people whose violence against him he has experienced. Let him altogether commit himself afresh to the apostolic and catholic creed up to and including the meeting of the synod of Nicea. By this acknowledgement, light and lax though it seems to some, he is to recover what he has lost through the guile of the leadership. Yet if anyone is found to be so dull of mind (which I do not think will happen) as not only to refuse to be converted by receiving the health-giving remedy, but in his guilty state believes the poisonous disease will rescue him, he will be constrained by reason, handed over without recovery to the author of perfidy, and he will be punished by the spiritual strength of the Catholic Church. *Here it ends.*

---

[1] No III, Para. 2: *Here it ends*] Scribe's note.

[IV]¹ /p.158/ *Copy of the letter of the bishops of Italy.*

To the dearly beloved brothers holding the fathers' faith throughout Illyricum, eternal salvation in the Lord from the bishops of Italy.

1.² It is a work of divine grace that we have begun all to be of one mind, all to confess one thing [Phil 2:2], in accordance with the Apostle. The whole extent of Italy, indeed, has returned to the fathers' faith of old, that is to the creed written at Nicea, recognizing the fraud that faith had suffered at Rimini. We rejoice, too, that God has taken thought, in his clement will, for Illyricum; the fellowship of unbelief with which it was burdened has been cast aside and we are glad that it has begun to approve those things which are of right opinion. Do you therefore, dearly beloved brothers, take our one and the same sentence and affirm it with your subscription. We preserve the decrees of the Nicene proceedings against Arius and Sabellius by whose shared inheritance Fotinus is condemned. We rescind by law the council of Rimini's decrees (corrupted, as they had been, by the shiftiness of certain persons) with the agreement of all the provinces. We have decided too that copies of these should be conveyed so that there should be seen to be no disagreement on the faith being maintained or in the rebuttal of the council of Rimini. Whoever wants to have fellowship in our unity of mind, and whoever desires to be in undivided peace with us, should quickly ratify our decisions by sending their subscription to the creed we have mentioned and an unequivocal rescinding of the council of Rimini. We are assured in our request, because we ourselves present it with the agreement of the majority of these provinces. But /p. 159/ it is plain that the instigators of the Arian or Aëtian heresy, Valens and Ursacius and the rest of the associates of these same people, have not been condemned now just because they have begun to manifest themselves in Illyricum, but were condemned long ago. *Here it ends.*

---

¹ No IV, Heading: *Copy...Italy*] Excerptor's note.
² No IV, Para. 1: *Here it ends*] Scribe's note.

[V]¹ /p.47/ *The letter of Germinius against the Arians who had subscribed at the council of Rimini, conscious of their wrong-doing.*

I, Germinius, bishop, do believe and profess that there is one true God the Father, eternal, omnipotent. And that Christ is his only Son and our Lord God, true Son of God from true God the Father, begotten before all things; in Godhead, love, majesty, power, splendour, life, wisdom and knowledge, like in all things to the Father, as perfect offspring from the perfect. The assumption, too, of man from the Virgin Mary, as the prophets predicted it would come to pass and the /p. 48/ words of the evangelists and the apostles teach us it has been fulfilled, his suffering too and death, his resurrection and ascension to heaven - these we accept, believe and profess; and also that he will descend from heaven at the end of the world to judge quick and dead and to recompense each according to his deeds. And we believe in the Holy Ghost, that is the Paraclete, who has been given us by God the Father through the Son.

[VI]² /p. 159/ *A copy of the letter of Valens, Ursatius and the others to Germinius.*

Valens, Ursacius, Gaius and Paul to the most religious lord and brother Germinius.

1.³ Since concern for faith and salvation weighs heavy upon us, those who feel the concern ought to be praised rather than suffer a reproof for it. Salvation, however, and hope reside first and foremost in the Catholic faith. And so, although you had been advised by our lord brothers and fellow bishops, Valens and Paul at your meeting with them to respond

---

¹ No V, Heading: *The letter of Germinius...wrong-dong*] Excerptor's note.
Para. 1: *Like in all things*] Sc. including substance.

² No VI, Heading: *A copy...Germinius*] Excerptor's heading.

³ Para. 1: *Basil's declaration of false faith*] I.e. Basil of Ancyra. See the anathematisms of his council at Ancyra, 358, in Hahn (op. cit. in note to Book Two no. VII Para. 2) no. 162. The claim is that if Basil had not insisted upon 'substance' appearing in any formal account of the faith, and persuaded the Emperor (temporarily) that this was the right course, all would have been well.

to the current rumour about you and refused to do so, nevertheless, most religious sir, because you testified in your letter that you continue in that same love towards us and are prepared to maintain and show us your unimpaired regard, we, in united assembly at Singidunum, hereby jointly repeat our advice to your Holiness that you should rule out any opportunity for doubt by writing back again to us. You are asked to signify more openly that you will not depart from the Catholic faith expounded and confirmed by the holy council at Rimini, to which creed all the bishops of the East gave their united assent, as you yourself have already acknowledged. However, there is in that creed the following provision: we call the Son 'like the Father in accordance with the scriptures' not 'like in substance; ' or 'like in all things' but 'like' without further qualification. For if this expression is altered, clearly Basil's declaration of false faith, which /p. 160/ produced the synod and which was deservedly condemned, will be restored.

2. Please, therefore, do as we ask and declare plainly in your letter that you did not, do not, and will not, say he is 'like the Father in all things except ingeneracy', in case what the bearers of this letter, Jovian the deacon and Martirius the subdeacon, asserted, with a word of deprecation in front of my aforesaid brothers and fellow-bishops Valens and Paul, should seem more credible: that you profess the Son 'like the Father in all things'. For if, as we hope, you make it plain by your letter that this is your view, the complaint of misconduct made by certain of your clergy, to our brothers and fellow bishops Palladius and Gaius (though you refused to examine it, as you were advised to do at the first meeting) has no bearing upon your reputation and they will answer for their unfounded charge. We have despatched this to your Charity, through Secundianus the presbyter, Pullentius the reader, and Candidian the exorcist, XV Kal. Jan. in the consulship of the most noble Gratian and Dagalaifus, retaining a copy for ourselves.

[VII][1] /p.161/ *Here begins Germinius' letter in answer to Rufianus, Palladius and the rest.*

---

[1] No. VII, Heading: *Here begins...rest*] Excerptor's note.

Greetings in the Lord from Germinius to his lords and most religious brothers Rufianus, Palladius, Severinus, Nichas, Heliodorus, Romulus, Mucianus and Stercorius.

1.[1] We have discovered by the report of Vitalis, currently a serving officer in the exalted prefecture, that your holinesses desire it should be /p.161/ openly signified to you what it is that Valens, Ursacius, Gaius and Paul took exception to in our creed. I have thought it necessary to make plain in this letter to your holinesses and to state what I am confident has been in your minds from the beginning. We ourselves accept what was delivered to us by the fathers and divine scriptures, what we learned once and teach daily: Christ, the Son of God, our Lord, is like the Father in all things except ingeneracy, God from God, light from light, power from power, whole from whole, perfect from perfect, begotten before the ages and before all things which can be thought about and spoken of. His birth no one knows save the Father, since the Son himself declares: 'No one has known the Son except the Father, nor does anyone know the Father except the Son and him to whom the Son has willed to reveal him' [Matt 11:27]. All things were made through him and without him nothing was made [Cf. Jn 1:3], according to the divine words of our Saviour himself who says: 'Up to now my Father works and I work' [Jn 5:17]; and again: 'For whatever things the Father does, the Son does likewise' [Jn 5:19]; and again: 'The Father and I are one' [Jn 10:30]; and again: 'He who has seen me has seen the Father too' [Jn 14:9]; and again: :'Just as the Father has life in himself, so has he granted the Son to have life in himself' [Jn 5:26]; and again: 'Just as the Father raises and quickens the dead, so too the Son quickens whom he wills' [Jn 5:21]; and again: 'Believe in God, believe also in me' [Jn 14:1]; and again: 'For neither does the Father judge anyone, but he has given all judgement to the Son, that all may honour the Son as they honour the Father' [Jn 5:2f]. And again, to whom is it that the Father said: 'Let us make man in our image and likeness'? [Gen 1:26] He did not say 'in your image' or 'in my image', in case it might point to some unlikeness in his own Son's Godhead. No, he added 'in our image and likeness', to /p. 162/ make it plain that his own Son is God,

---

[1] Para. 1: ...*currently*...] Reading 'nunc' instead of 'v.c' [=vir clarissimus, 'high-ranking'].

like him in all things. Again, the Evangelist says: 'We saw his glory, glory as of the Only-begotten of the Father, full of grace and truth' [Jn 1:4]. And the Apostle says to the Corinthians: 'In whom the god of this world has blinded the minds of unbelievers, so that they should not shine with the illumination of the gospel of the glory of Christ which is the image of God' [2 Cor 4:4]. And again the Apostle says: 'And he has transferred us to the kingdom of his Son's love, in whom we have redemption, remission of sins, he who is the image of the invisible God, first begotten of all creation' [Col 1:13ff]. And again the same Apostle says: 'Have this mind in you which also was in Christ Jesus, who, though he was in the form of God, thought it no booty to be equal with God but emptied himself, taking a slave's form, being made in the likeness of men' [Phil 2:5ff]. is there anybody who does not understand that just as our veritable flesh was in Christ in accordance with the 'slave's form', so also the veritable Godhead of the Father is in the Son in 'the form of God'? And again: 'See to it that nobody leads you astray through philosophy and empty deceit in accordance with men's teaching, in accordance with the elements of the world, and not in accordance with Christ; because in him dwells all the fulness of the Godhead bodily' [Col 2:8f]. If, therefore, the 'fulness of the Godhead' dwells in Christ, then they are not partly like and partly unlike as is asserted by people who retreat and turn aside from us owing to their lust for quarreling.

2. For because they think they are doing something grand by quoting the divine scriptures when these call Christ 'made' [Acts 2:36; Hab 3:14] and 'creature' [Prov 8:22], we, on the contrary /p. 163/ call him, in accordance with the scriptures, 'way' [Jn 14:6], 'door' [Jn 10:7], 'stone of stumbling and rock of offence' [Is 8:14; Rom 8:33], 'foundation' [1 Cor 3:11], 'arm' [Is 51:9; Lk 1:151; Jn 12:38 etc], 'hand' [Ex 13:9b etc], 'wisdom' [1 Cor 1:24, 30], 'word' [Jn 1:1, 14 etc], 'lamb' [Jn 1:29 etc], 'sheep' [Is 53:7; Acts 8:32], shepherd' [Jn 10:11, 14], 'priest' [Heb 5:6.], 'vine' [Jn 15:1, 5], 'day' [Mal 4:1] and the rest. But all these we understand and call him, meaning powers and operations of God's Son, and not in order to put his divine birth from the Father on a footing with names of this kind; because all things were made from nothing through the Son, whereas the Son was not begotten from nothing but from God the Father.

3. I am, however, surprised that the aforesaid Valens has either forgotten or is assuredly giving a cunning disguise to what was done and determined in the past. For in the reign of Constantius of good memory, there was a time when a disagreement between certain people on the faith had started up. Under the gaze of the Emperor himself, in the presence of George bishop of the church of Alexandria, of Pancratius bishop of Pelusium, of Basil then bishop of Anquira, in the presence too of Valens himself, of Ursacius and of my unimportant self, after a disputation on the faith which lasted till nightfall, Marcus was chosen by us all to draw up a creed composed according to a fixed pattern. The following was written in that creed: 'The Son is like the Father in all things, as the holy scriptures say and teach'; and we all agreed to this full profession of faith and signed it with our own hands. But if the spirit of this world is now prompting them to something, we have not been able so far to get a clear knowledge of it. For seeing how we ourselves professed 'the Son is like the Father in all things except ingeneracy' on the basis of the scriptures, let them explain from the scriptures in what way he is partly like, partly unlike.

4. /p. 164/ And so, dearly beloved brothers, I have despatched this declaration without hesitation or delay for the common knowledge of your Charities, through Cyriacus the officer, this being the first available opportunity after I sent Carinius the deacon to you. I have sent it so that, through your most vigilant devotion to God, it may be made known to all the brotherhood, in case anyone in ignorance of it may be caught up in the toils of the deceitful Devil [cf. 2 Tim 2:26]. It belongs to your unanimous selves to write back what the Holy Ghost prompts you to. However, I let your Charities know that I have been unable to sign this letter, because I have a pain in my hand and have ordered a signing by our brothers and fellow presbyters Innocentius, Octavius and Catulus. *Here it ends.*[1]

---

[1] Para. 4. *Here it ends*] Excerptor's note.

/p.197/ Saint Hilary's *LETTER TO THE EMPEROR CONSTANTIUS,*
WHICH HE HIMSELF DELIVERED AT CONSTANTINOPLE:
(LIBER II AD CONSTANTIUM).[1]

1. I am not unaware, most devout Emperor, that addresses for the
knowledge of a public audience on a number of subjects are usually
considered either serious or trifling according to the worthiness of their
authors, as disregard or favour for the person moves the fluctuating
judgement of divided opinion, the while, to an exercise of the
understanding. But I have no fear of popular usage, when I shall speak,
in your presence, devout words on a divine theme; because, since you
are good and religious, amongst those who take thought for religious
matters even misjudgement does not determine what it hears by whom
it hears, but whether what it hears are religious. And, because God has
afforded me the opportunity of your presence, the office of my
conscience has not ceased with regard to these things, so that some
unworthiness perhaps of the one who speaks with you may offend
against the word of religion which I have in your presence.

2.[2] I am a bishop /p. 198/ in communion with all the churches and
bishops of the Gauls, and, though in exile, I continue a bishop and have
been administering communion through my presbyters. Yet I am exiled
not by an offence, but by a faction and by a synod's false messengers
to you, devout Emperor, impeached, as I am, by impious men with no
knowledge of guilty acts on my part. I have a witness of no light weight
to my complaint in my religious lord Julian, your Caesar, who has
endured through my exile more of calumny from the malicious than I
of injustice; indeed, your Piety's letters are here at hand. But all the
falsehoods of those who procured them for my exile are evident. The
agent and author of all the events is also within this city. Let me rely
on that state of my knowledge and disclose that you, Augustus, have
been cheated and your Caesar deceived, so that if I am proved to have
done anything unworthy, not just of the sanctity of a bishop but of the

---

[1] Heading: *Letter...Constantinople*] Scribal heading. It is called a *liber*; it is not an official
letter (it has no formal address) but an 'open letter' to be read by the Emperor but for
public discussion too.

[2] Para. 2: *Julian*] Born 331, made Caesar 335 and assigned to Gaul; proclaimed Augustus
at Paris 360.

integrity of a layman, I may look for no priesthood by pardon but may grow old in the state of a penitent layman.

3. But now, most courteous Emperor, I leave to your decision how far, and in what way, you bid me speak of these things, and will go on to those matters which most require to be done with you now. You will allow me, indeed, to set out the case by bringing forward at once the man in person by whose agency I am in exile, even to the point of his confessing the falsehoods he has committed. But I will say nothing of him unless you bid me. But now I say that I fear the world's peril, guilty silence on my part, God's judgement; yet that my concern is for hope, life, and immortality: not so much mine as yours and all men's. This concern I say I share with very many /p. 199/ and so it is the expectation of shared hope.

4. Recognize the faith which of old, best and most religious Emperor, you have been desiring to hear from bishops and do not hear! For whilst those it is sought from write their own words and do not preach God, they have revolved an endless cycle of error and ever-returning strife. A proper sense of human weakness demanded that the whole mystery of divine knowledge should be contained only within those bounds of its own consciousness to which it has entrusted it, and that after the confessed and sworn baptismal faith in the name of the Father, Son and Holy Ghost [Matt 28:19], there should be no further doubt or innovation. But the presumption, opportunism or error of certain persons has in part made a hypocritical profession of the unchangeable structure of apostolic teaching and in part boldly departed from it, whilst in the confession of Father, Son and Holy Ghost belying the natural significance, lest anything confessed in the sacrament of rebirth remain in its true meaning. so, in the consciousness of certain persons the Father is not Father, the Son not Son, the Holy Ghost not Holy Ghost. The custom then became fixed, by the allegedly objectionable occasion of necessity, of writing and innovating in the creed. After custom began to create the new, rather than hold to the accepted, it neither defended the ancient nor confirmed the innovated and the creed came to belong to the times rather than the gospels, being written in accordance with the years and not maintained in accordance with the baptismal confession. It is a /p. 200/ very dangerous and lamentable thing that we

now have as many creeds as we have wills, as many teachings as we have customs, and that as many occasions for blasphemies sprout up as there are vices, whilst creeds are either written as we will or interpreted as we do not will. And though there is one faith (as there is one God, one Lord, one baptism [cf. Eph 4:5] we have departed from that faith which is the only one. And the more there have begun to be, the more they have begun to amount to a non-existence of creeds.

5.[1] For after the meeting of the synod at Nicea we are aware of nothing other than our taking turns in writing the faith. Meanwhile there is verbal battle, dispute about novelties, opportunity for doubts, complaint about authors, struggle over aims, difficulty in agreement; there begins to be anathema against anathema, and almost nobody belongs to Christ. We wander in an uncertain wind of doctrines [cf. Eph 4:14] and either disturb when we teach or go astray when we are taught. Indeed, what change does last year's faith contain? The first creed decrees no mention of 'omousion'; the second decrees and re-proclaims 'omousion'; next, the third /p. 201/ absolves the fathers for the 'usia' they ventured in simple fashion; finally, the fourth does not absolve but condemns them. Where have we got to at long last? To the point where nothing any more stays sacred and inviolable with us or anybody before us. But if the wretched faith of our time is about the likeness of God the Son to God the Father, so that he should not be like either wholly or only partially, we, the illustrious, indeed, umpires of heavenly mysteries, we scrutineers of invisible mysteries, falsely blame the professions of faith in God. We determine 'faiths' about God yearly and monthly; we do penance for the decrees, we defend the penitent, we anathematize those defended, we condemn either what is different in ours or ours in the

---

[1] Para. 5: *Meanwhile...agreement*] Cf. Ferrandus *Letter to Pelagius and Anatolius* PL 67,922.
ibid.: *Indeed...but condemns them.*] The four creeds are: (1) the 'Blasphemy' of Sirmium (357) = Hahn (op. cit. in note to Book Two no. VII Para. 2); (2) the declaration of the Catholics at Rimini (see Book Two no. XII); (3) The creed of Nice (see Book Two no. XVII and synposis) which is given in Hahn no. 164: it speaks of the Fathers' 'somewhat naive' use of the term *usia* which is now disowned; (4) Finally, the creed now proposed at Constantinople (Hahn no. 167): it is identical with that of Nice, save for the condemnation of 'all the heresies, ancient and modern, opposed to the present document' sc. including all who had (mis)used the term *usia*.

different creeds; and as we bite one another [cf. Gal 5:15] we are annihilated by one another.

6. Faith is asked for, as if no faith existed. A faith is written down, as if it were not in the heart. We who have been reborn by faith are now instructed as to the faith, as if that rebirth were without faith. We are instructed in Christ after baptism, as if there could be any baptism without Christ's faith. We correct it, as if it were pardonable to sin against the Holy Ghost [cf. Matt 12:32]. The chief and lasting cause of irreligion, however, is that though we bring forward the apostolic faith seven times over we refuse ourselves to confess the gospel faith, as we publicly defend our impieties meanwhile with newfangled chatter, deluding the ears of the simple with bombast and deceptive words, as we avoid believing about the Lord Jesus Christ what /p. 202/ he taught us to believe, as we surreptiously unite under the specious name of peace, claim to reject novelties whilst rebelling again against God with new terms, and use the text of the scriptures to invent things that are not in the scriptures. Errant, impious spendthrifts, we all the while change things abiding, waste the gifts received and venture things irreligious.

7. The safe principle observed by seafarers in a storm on a billowy sea, to go back to the harbour they sailed from when a hurricane blows, applies to careless young people too. Left to look after their house, they use their freedom to excess and overstep due regard for their father. If they fear to lose the estate, their only safe and needful course is a return to the father's ways. Thus, amidst these shattered ruins of the ship of faith, with the legacy of the heavenly estate well nigh now squandered, the safest thing for us to do is to keep hold of the first and only gospel faith confessed and understood at baptism and not change the only thing I have received and heard; to be assured that what a synod of our forebears maintained is not to be damned as an irreligious and impious document, but that it is misused by human presumption for contradiction, which is why the Gospel is denied in the name of novelty and risky alleged new improvements are hence produced. Improvement is always progressive. Every improvement is found unsatisfactory and the next improvement damns every other improvement. Whatever the point, there is never an improvement on an improvement but it starts being a damnation.

8. /p. 203/ How I admire you, lord Constantius, as a man of blessed and religious will who yearns for a creed only according to the scriptures! Very rightly do you haste towards those utterances of the Only-begotten God so that the breast holding an emperor's cares may be full with the awareness of divine words. He who rejects this is anti-Christ, he who feigns it is anathema. Yet one thing I beg of you at this courteous and frank hearing: at the synod now taking place and quarreling about the faith, be good enough to hear a few words of mine on the gospels and let me speak with you of the words of Jesus Christ my Lord, whose exiled priest I am. For earthen vessels contain noble treasures[cf. 2 Cor 4:7] and frailer bodies are the more respected. And with us, indeed, uneducated fishermen spoke of God. According to the prophet, God has regard to the humble man who trembles at his words [cf. Is 66:2]. You seek a faith, Emperor. Hear it, not from new pamphlets, but God's books. Know that it can be granted in the West too, whence they shall come and recline with Abraham, Isaac and Jacob in God's kingdom [cf. Matt 8:11]. Remember it does not exist in a debate on philosophy but in the teaching of the Gospel. Not so much for my sake do I beg a hearing, as for yourself and God's churches. I have a faith within, I need no external one. What I have received I keep and do not change, because it is God's.

9. /p.204/ However, you are to remember that there is none of the heretics who falsely says he does not now preach the terms of his blasphemies in accordance with the scriptures. Marcellus is thus unaware of 'the Word of God' [Jn 1:1] when he reads it. Thus Fotinus is ignorant when he says 'the man Jesus Christ' [Rom 5:15]. Hence too Sabellius, when he does not understand 'the Father and I are one' [Jn 10:30], is without God the Father and without God the Son. Hence too Montanus used his mad women to defend 'other Paraclete' [Jn 14:16.] Hence too Manicheus and Marcion hate the law because 'the letter kills' [2 Cor 3:6] and the Devil is the 'prince of this world' [Jn 12:31]. They speak the scriptures without scripture's meaning; they put forward a faith without faith. For the scriptures do not consist in reading, but in being understood; not in quibbling but in charity.

10. Hear, I beg you, what the Bible says of Christ, lest what it does not say be preached instead. Bend your ears to what I shall say from the scriptures. Lift up your faith towards God. Hearken to what conduces to faith, unity, eternity. I shall speak with you words which conduce to the peace of East and West along with the honour of the realm and your own faith. I shall speak them subject to public knowledge, with a synod divided, with a court-case notorious.

11. Meanwhile I give a guarantee of my future speech in your presence. I will not advocate anything to cause offence, anything outside the Gospel.

You will understand that in the sacred mystery of 'the sole true God' [Jn 17:3] and 'Jesus Christ whom he sent' [ibid.], one God the Father is preached 'from whom are all things' [1 Cor 8:6] /p. 205/ and one Lord Jesus Christ 'through whom are all things' [ibid.], who is born from God, is 'before eternal times' [2 Tim 1:9] and was 'in the beginning with God' [Jn 1:1], God 'the Word' [ibid.], 'who is the image of the invisible of God' [Col 1:15], in whom 'the whole fulness of the Godhead dwells bodily' [Col 2:9], who 'though he was in the form of God' humbled himself for our salvation and took 'slave's form' [Phil 2:6] [Phil 2:7.] in virgin's conception by the Holy Ghost, 'being made obedient to death, but the death of a cross' [Phil 2:8], and after resurrection from the dead is seated 'in the heavens' [Eph 1:20] and will be present as 'judge of quick and dead' [Acts 10:42] and 'king of all eternal ages' [Rev 15:3]. For he is 'Only-begotten God' [Jn 1:18], 'true God' [1 Jn 5:20.] and 'great God' [Titus 2:13], God over all' [Rom 9:5] and 'every tongue will confess that Jesus Christ is Lord in the glory of God the Father' [Phil 2:11]. These things have I believed on in the Holy Ghost, in such wise that beyond this faith concerning the Lord Jesus Christ I cannot be instructed. Hereby I do not reduce the religion our fathers believed, but in accordance with the creed of my rebirth and the knowledge of the teaching of the Gospel, I am, with these teachings as my standard, in accord with it.

SELECT BIBLIOGRAPHY

1. The sources.

These are primarily the works of Athanasius, and the *Church Histories* of Socrates, Sozomen and Theodoret together with Hilary himself and Epiphanius the hereseologist. (References, in Introduction and annotations, to these and to the other texts of Christian writers of the period use the Clavis number preceded by CPG or CPL: ed. M. Geerard *Clavis Patrum Graecorum* (Turnhout, 1974ff); ed. E. Dekkers/S. Gaar *Clavis Patrum Latinorum* (Bruges, 1961). They are an indispensable guide to editions). Modern English translations of most of these are available in the series *Nicene and post-Nicene Fathers* (reprinted Grand Rapids,1960ff).

2. Modern literature and studies.

Standard histories of the Church in this period are:
H. Chadwick *The Early Church* (Harmondsworth, 1967).
    ed. A. Fliche and V.Martin *Histoire de l'Église* vol. 3 (Paris, 1947): De la Paix Constantinienne à la mort de Théodose.
    ed. H. Jedin and J. Dolan trans. A. Biggs *History of the Church* vol. 2 (London, 1980): The Imperial Church from Constantine to the Early Middle Ages.
    For the 'Arian' controversy in all its ramifications the latest full-length study is:
    R.P.C. Hanson *The search for the Christian Doctrine of God*: The Arian controversy 318 - 381(Edinburgh, 1988).
    R.Lorenz in *Das vierte Jahrhundert (Osten)* = vol, 1, fascicle C2 of *Die Kirche in ihrer Geschichte: Ein Handbuch* ed. B.Moeller (Göttingen, 1992) conveniently summarizes the various aspects of Church life in the East, with references to both the ancient sources and modern studies.
    Two studies are of particular note for Hilary and these texts:
H.C.Brennecke *Hilarius von Poitiers und die Bischofsopposition gegen Konstantius II*: Untersuchungen zur dritten Phase des arianischen Streites (337-361).

P. Smulders *Hilary of Poitiers' Preface to his* Opus Historicum: Translation and Commentary (Leiden/New York/Köln, 1995).
Both works contain excellent bibliographies.

Fundamental for the study of these texts was the work of A.Feder whose Praefatio to his edition is a mine of information, as are his Studien I and II zu Hilarius von Poitiers in Sitzungsberichte der kaiserlichen Akademie der Wissenschaften Phil-Hist. Klasse 162.4 and 166.5 (Vienna, 1910 and 1911).

Reverse index of the fragments as printed in Feder's edition

Series A	I		Book Three I
	II		Book Three II
	III		Book Three V
	IV	1	
		2	Book One II
		3	
	V	1	Book Two XIV
		2	Book Two XV
		3	Book Two XVI
		4	Book Two XVII
	VI		Book Two XVIII
	VII		Book Two III
	VIII		Book Two XI
	IX	1	Book Two XII
		2	Book Two XIII
		3	
Series B	I		Book One I
	II	1	Book One III
		2	
		3	Book One IV
		4	
		5	Book One V
		6	Book One VI
		7	
		8	Book One VII

			9		Book One VIII
Series B	II		10		Book One IX
			11		
	III		1	('Studens paci')	Book Two I
			2		Book Two II
	IV		1	('Imperitiae culpam')	Book Three III
			2		Book Three IV
	V				Book Three VI
	VI				Book Three VII
	VII		1		Book Two IV
			2	('Quamvis sub imagine')	
			3		Book Two V
			4	('Nolo te')	
			5		Book Two VI
			6	('Inter haec')	
			7		Book Two VII
			8	('Pro deifico')	
			9		Book Two VIII
			10	('Quia scio')	Book Two IX
			11	('Non doceo')	Book Two X
	VIII		1		Book Two XIX
			2		Book Two XX

Oratio Synodi Sardicensis ad Imperatorem Constantium Imperatorem et textus narrativus
S. Hilarii (Liber I ad Constantium)-

| 1 - 5 | Book One X |
| 6 - 8 | Book One XI |

Index of personal names occurring in the text

[Names asterisked have an entry in the *Encyclopedia of the Early Church*, ed. Angelo di Berardino, Cambridge 1992 (translated by Adrian Walford from *Dizionario Patristico e di Antichità Cristiane*)]

Abraham, biblical patriarch 15, 108
*Acacius, bishop of Caesarea in Palestine 38, 46, 47, 50, 67, 78
Adamantius, bishop of Cius 40
Aët(h)ius, bishop of T(h)essalonica 32, 51
*Aëtius, anomean heretic 89
Agapius, bishop of T(h)enus 40
*Alexander, bishop of Alexandria 45, 73
Alexander (bishop) of Ciparissia 52
Alexander (bishop) of Coroni [?] 52
Alexander (bishop) of Larissa 51
Alypius (bishop) of Megara 51
Ambracius, bishop of Miletus 40
*Amfion, bishop of Nicomedia 20
Ammonius, bishop 44
Annianus (bishop) of Castolona 50
Antonius, bishop of Bosra 41
Antonius, bishop of Docimium 38
Antonius, bishop of Zeuma 38
Arcydamus, presbyter (of Rome) 48
Arius (bishop), of Palestine 46, 51
*Ar(r)ius, heretic/two Ar(r)iuses 60, 67, 73, 74, 98
Arians/Ariomaniacs 55, 57, 60, 68, 71, 79, 93, 96
*Arsenius, alleged victim of Athanasius 44
Arsenius (bishop) 89
Arthemius, bishop 86
*Asclepius/Asclepas, bishop of Gaza 26, 27, 28, 33, 33, 42, 53, 45, 46, 50
*Asterius (bishop) of Arabia 51
*Athanasius, bishop of Alexandria 18, 24, 25, 26, 27, 28, 29, 30, 32, 33, 35, 36, 41, 42, 43, 44, 45, 46, 48, 50, 51, 52, 53, 54, 55, 56, 57, 58, 59, 64, 67, 68, 69, 70, 71, 72, 73, 74, 77, 79, 80
Athenodorus, (bishop) of Elatea 51

*Auxentius (bishop of Milan) 79, 94

*Basil, bishop of An(qu)c(i)yra) 39, 46, 78, 100, 103
Bassus, bishop of Carpathus 40, 78
Bassus (bishop) of Diocletianopolis 31, 50
Bitinicus, bishop of Zela 39

Caecilian, bishop of Spoleto 76
Calepodius, (bishop) of Naples 51
*Callinicus, bishop of Pelusium 40
Calvus (bishop) of Castramartis 51
Candidian, exorcist (of Illyricum) 100
Carinius, deacon (of Illyricum) 103
Cartherius, bishop of Aspona 39
Castus (bishop) of Caesarea Augusta 50
Catulus (bishop, of Illyricum) 103
Cecropius (bishop of Nicomedia) 78
*Constantine, Emperor 2, 71, 83, 84
*Constantius, Emperor 64, 65, 71, 77, 79, 80, 83, 87, 89, 103, 108
Cresconius, bishop 40
Cyriacus (bishop) of Naisus 22, 36
Cyriacus, an officer 103
Cyrotus, bishop of Rosus 38

Dagalaifus, consul 100
David, king 23
*Demofilus, bishop of Beroe 49, 73, 77, 78
Desiderius, bishop, of Campania 20
Dianius, bishop of Caesarea (in Cappadocia) 38
Didimion (bishop) 89
Diodorus (bishop) of Tenedos 51
Diogenes, bishop 40
Diognitus=Theognitus
Dionisius, bishop of Alexandria (in Cilicia) 39
Dionisius (bishop) of Elida 31, 51
*Dionisius, bishop of Milan 69, 75
Dioscorus (bishop) of Terasia 51
Dominius (bishop) of Polidiane [?] 39

Domitianus (bishop) of Asturica Spaniarum 50
Donatus, bishop of Carthage 20

Ecdicius (bishop) [of Pernasus?] 89
Edesius, bishop of Cous 40
Eliodorus (bishop) of Nicopolis 51
Eortasius (bishop) [of Sardis] [?] 89
Epictetus (bishop of Centumcellae) 71, 79, 87
Erodianus (bishop) 88
Evagrius (bishop) of Eraclia Linci 51
Evagrius (bishop) 78
Eucarpius (bishop) 89
Eudemon, bishop of T(h)anis 40
Eudemon, bishop 40
*Eudoxius, bishop of Germanicia 39, 73, 78
Eugenius, bishop 41
Eugeus, bishop of Lisinia 38
Eulalius, bishop of Amasias 38
Eumatius (legate) 88
*Eusebius, bishop (of Nicomedia, later of Constantinople) 42, 45
*Eusebius (bishop) of Caesarea (in Palestine) 45
Eusebiuses, two (= bishop of Caesarea + namesake of Nicomedia) 45,
    67
Eusebius, bishop of Dorilaium 39
Eusebius, bishop of Magnesia 39
Eusebius, bishop of Pergamum (in Asia) 39
Eusebius, bishop of Pergamum (in Thrace[?]) 40
*Eusebius, (bishop) of Vercelli 69, 75, 95, 96
Eusebius (bishop) 72
Eusebius, consul 81, 82, 86
*Eustas(th)ius (bishop of Antioch) 36
Eustat(h)ius (bishop) of Epiphania 39
Eut(h)erius, bishop (of Sirmium) of the Pannonias 51
Eut(h)erius, (bishop) of Gannos 50
Euthicius, bishop, of Campania 20
Euticius, (bishop) of Motoni 52
Euticius, bishop of Filippopolis 41
Exuperantius (bishop) 78

Filetus,. bishop of Cratia 39
Filetus, bishop of Juliopolis 39
Filoxenus, presbyter (of Rome) 48
Flaccus, bishop of (H)Ieropolis (in Phrygia) 40
Florentius, bishop of Ancyra 40
Florentius (bishop) of Emerita 50
*Fortunatianus (bishop), of Aquileia 51, 71, 77, 79
Fortunatus, bishop of Naples 20
*Fotinus, bishop of Sirmium 54, 56, 58, 108

Gaius (bishop, of Illyricum) 83, 84, 86, 88, 94, 99, 101
Gaudentius (bishop) of Naisus 35, 36, 51
Gaudentius (bishop) 78
*George, bishop of Alexandria 73, 103
*George (bishop) of La(u)od(o)icia) 45, 47, 50
*Germinius (bishop of Sirmium) 78, 83, 84, 86, 88, 99, 100
Geroncius (bishop) of Bereu (in Macedonia) 52
Gerontius, bishop of Raphania 38
Gratian, consul 100
Grecianus, bishop of Calle 82
*Gregory, bishop of Alexandria 46
*Gregory, bishop (of Elvira) of Spain 95, 96
Gregory, (bishop) 86

Helianus, presbyter (Rome) 70
Heliodorus - see Eliodorus
Heliodorus (bishop, of Illyricum) 101
Helpidius (bishop of Satala[?] in Armenia) 88
Heortasius - see Eortasius
Herodianus - see Erodianus
*Hilary, bishop of Poitiers/Pictavium 78, 93, 95
Hilary, deacon (of Rome) 75
Hilary, eunuch 79
Himenius (bishop) of Ypata 51
Hireneus (bishop) 78
Honoratus (1), (bishop) 86
Honoratus (2), (bishop) 86
Hyginus, Hypatius - see Yginus, Ypatius

Innocentius (bishop, of Illyricum) 103
Irenaeus - see Ireneus, Hireneus
Ireneus (bishop) of Scirus 51
Isaac, biblical patriarch 108
Isaac, bishop of Letus 40
Ischyras/ Scyras/Scyrus/Squirius bishop (of Mareotis) 24, 39, 44, 45, 52,
      53

Jacob, biblical patriarch 108
Januarius (bishop) of Beneventum 51
Jonas (bishop) of Particopolis 51
Jovian, deacon (of Illyricum) 100
*Julian, Caesar 104
*Julius, bishop of Rome 27, 28, 33, 35, 36, 44, 47, 53, 54, 55, 70, 71,
      77
Julius (bishop) of T(h)ebes (H)Eptapilos 51
Julius (bishop) 78
Junior (bishop) 78
Justin, bishop 86, 88, 94

Leo, deacon (of Rome) 48
Leontius (bishop) 89
Leucadas, bishop of Ilium 40
*Liberius, bishop of Rome 70, 71, 75, 76, 77, 78, 80, 96
*Lucifer, bishop of (Cagliari/Calaris in) Sardinia 69, 71, 74, 75
Lucius, bishop of Antinous 40
Lucius (bishop) of Adrianopolis 26, 27, 51
Lucius (bishop) of Verona 51
Lucius, bishop 86
Lucius, presbyter (of Rome) 70

Macarius, (bishop) 89
*Mac(h)edonius, bishop of Mopsuestia 36, 38, 73, 78
Mac(h)arius, presbyter (of Alexandria) 44, 53
Mac(h)edonius, bishop of Biritus 39
Machedonius (bishop) of Ulpiani 51
Ma(i)gdonius (legate) 87, 88
*Manicheus, heretic 108

*Marcellus (bishop) of Ancyra 21, 22, 23, 24, 26, 27, 28, 29, 30, 31, 32, 33, 35, 36, 37, 41, 42, 43, 43, 45, 46, 8, 50, 54, 57, 58, 76, 108
Marcellus, bishop from Campania
Marcialis, legate 88
*Marcion, heretic 108
*Marcus, bishop of Aret(h)usa 38, 103
Marcus (bishop) of Siscia 52
Marcus (bishop, opponent of Ossius) 36
Marcus (bishop) 78
*Maris (bishop of Chalcedon) 42
Martirius, subdeacon (of Illyricum) 101
Martyrius (bishop) of Naupactus 51
Martyrius, bishop 73
*Maximinus (bishop) of Triveri 28, 35, 36, 53
Maximus (bishop) of Luca 50
*Maximus, bishop of Salona 20
Megasius, bishop 87, 88, 94
*Melitius, bishop of Lycopolis 45
Menofantus (bishop) of Ephesus 38, 46, 47, 50, 67
*Montanus, heretic 21, 108
Moyses (bishop, of Egypt) 56
Mucianus (bishop, of Illyricum) 101
Mus(a)eus, (bishop) of Thebes (in Thessaly) 50
Mustacius (bishop) 86

*Narcissus, bishop of Neronias/Irenopolis in Cilicia 40, 45, 47, 50, 67, 78
Neo, (bishop) 88
Nestorius, bishop 41
Nichas (bishop, of Illyricum) 101
Niconius, bishop of Troas 40
Nonnius, bishop of La(u)od(o)icea 40
*Novatus (*Novatian?), schismatic 35

Octavius (bishop, of Illyricum) 103
Olympius, bishop of Doliche 38
Optatus, legate 88

*Ossius (bishop) of Cordoba in Spain 28, 29, 31, 33, 35, 36, 37, 42, 50,
      53, 76, 95

Palladius (bishop) of Dium 52
*Palladius (bishop of Ratiaria in Dacia) 101
Pancracius, presbyter (of Rome) 74
Pancratius bishop of Parnasus 39
Pancratius, bishop of Pelusium 103
Pantagatus, bishop of Attalia 40
Paregorius (bishop) of Scupi 51
Passinicus (bishop of Zela) 89
Patritius (bishop) 88
Paulinus, bishop, of Dacia 36
*Paulinus, bishop of Triveri 19, 69
Paul, apostle 15, 21, 22, 48, 54, 98, 101
*Paul, bishop of Constantinople 26, 27, 28, 31, 32, 33, 35, 36
*Paul (bishop) of Samosata 21, 23, 35, 37
Paul, bishop 38
Paul (bishop, of Illyricum) 99, 101
Paul, presbyter (of Rome) 70
Peter, apostle 48, 54
*Photinus, see Fotinus
Pison, bishop of Adana 39
Pison, bishop of Trocnada 39
Plutarcus (bishop) of Patras 51
Porfirius (bishop) of Filippi 50
*Potamius (bishop of Olisipo) 71
Praetextatus (bishop) of Barcilona 50
Primus, bishop 86
Priscus, bishop 86
Prohaeresius, bishop of Sinopa 39
Protasius (bishop) of Milan 51
Protogenes bishop of Sardica 22, 29, 31, 32, 33, 35, 51
Pullentius, reader (of Illyricum) 100

Quimatius (bishop) 36
Quint(c)ianus, bishop of Gaza 38, 46
Quirius, bishop of F(Ph)ladelf(ph)ia 39

*Restutus (= Restitutus) bishop of Carthage 86
Romulus (bishop, of Illyricum) 101
Rufianus (bishop, of Illyricum) 101

*Sabellius, heretic 21, 35, 37, 93, 98, 108
Sabinianus, bishop of Chadimena[?] 39
*Saturninus (bishop of Arles) 53, 95
Scyras/Scyrus see Ischyras
*Secundianus presbyter (of Illyricum) 100
Severinus (bishop, of Illyricum) 101
Severus, bishop of Gabula 41
*Severus (bishop) of Ravenna 51
*Silvanus (bishop of Tarsus) 78, 88
*Silvester (bishop of Rome) 73
Simplicius (bishop) 78
Sinferon, bishop 20
Sion, bishop (of Athribis) 40
Sisinnius, bishop of Perge 40
Socras (= Socrates) (bishop) of Asopofoebia [?] 51
*Sofronius (bishop of Pompeiopolis in Paphlagonia) 88
Solomon (King) 24
Solutor, bishop 26
Squirius see Ischyras
Stephen (bishop) [S. (bishop), of Arabia] of Arabia
Stephen, bishop of Antioch 38, 45, 47, 50, 67
Stercorius (bishop) of Canusium 51
Stercorius (bishop, of Illyricum) 101
Surinus (bishop) 78

Taurinus, bishop 86
Taurus, praetorian prefect 88
Terentianus (bishop) 78
Thelafius, bishop of Calchedonia 38
*Theodorus, bishop of Heraclia 38, 45, 47, 67, 78
Theodorus (legate) 88
Theodulus, bishop of Neocaesarea 40
Theodulus (bishop of Trajanopolis in Thrace) 43
Theogenes, bishop of Licia 40

The(Di)ognitus (bishop of Nicea) 42, 43
Theophilus (bishop of Castabola) 88
Thimotheus, bishop of Ancialus 41
Thimotheus, bishop 39
Timasarcus, bishop 39
Trifon (bishop) of Macaria [?]) 51

Urbanus, bishop 86
Urbicus, deacon 80
Ursacius (bishop) of Brixa 51
*Ursac(t)ius (bishop) of Singidunum 42, 46, 47, 49, 50, 53, 54, 55, 56,
    67, 78, 83, 84, 86, 88, 90, 94, 95, 98, 99, 101, 103

Valens, (bishop) of Iscus 52
*Valens, bishop of My(u)rsa 41, 42, 46, 47, 49, 50, 53, 54, 55, 56, 67,
    69, 78, 83, 84, 86, 87, 88, 90, 94, 95, 98, 99, 101, 103
Valentinus (bishop) 89
*Valentinus, heretic 35
Venerius, commissioner (*agens in rebus*) 80
Verissimus (bishop) of Lyons 52
Viator, bishop49
*Vincentius, bishop of Capua 51, 76, 80
Vitalis (bishop) of Aquae in Dacia Ripensis 51
Vitalis, bishop of Tyre 39
Vitalis, serving officer in the prefecture of Rome 101

Yginus (bishop) 86
Ypatius, consul 81, 82, 86

Zosimus (bishop) of Lignidus 51

Index of places named in the text

Ac(h)ai(e)a 31, 51, 52
Adana (in Cilicia) 39
Adrianopolis 26
Africa 20, 41, 72
Alexandria 20, 25, 26, 31, 41, 46, 51, 64, 70, 71, 73, 103
Alexandria (in Cilicia) 39
Amasias (in Helenopontus) 38
Ancialus (in Haemimontus) 41
Ancy(qui)ra in Galatia [= modern Ankara] 26, 39, 41, 46, 50, 103
Ancyra in Lydia 51
Antinous (in the Thebaid) 40
Antioch (in Syria) [= modern Antakya] 38, 45, 50
Apulia 51
Aquae in Dacia Ripensis 51
Aquileia in Italy 49, 51, 56, 76
Arabia 20, 46, 51
Arles(Arelas) 19, 69, 72
Aret(h)usa (in Syria) 38
Asia, province 20, 46, 51
Asofoebia(?) in (Achaea) 51
Aspona (in Galatia) 39
Asturica Spaniarum 50
Attalia (in Lydia) 40

Barcilona 50
Beneventum 51
Bereu (= Beroea) in Mac(h)edonia 52
Beroe (in Thrace) 41
Biritus (in Phoenicia) 39
Biterrae [= modern Béziers] 18
Bithynia/Bitynia/Bitinia 20, 25
Bosra (Bostra) (in Arabia) 41
Brixa in Italy 51

Caesarea (in Cappadocia) 38

Caesarea in Palestine 25, 38, 45, 46, 50
Caesarea Augusta Spaniarum 50
Cainopolis (= Adrianopolis) in Thrace 51
Calchedonia (in Syria) (= Calchis?) 38
Calle (in Umbria) 82
Campania 20, 51, 76, 80
Canusium in Apulia 51
Cappadocia 20
Capua in Campania 51, 76
Caria 20
Carpathus (in the Cyclades) 40
Carthage 20
Castolona Spaniarum 50
Castramartis in Dacia Ripensis 51
Chadimena(??) (in Phrygia) 39
Cilicia 20, 45
Ciparissia in Ac(h)a(i)ea 52
Cius (in Bithynia) 40
Constantinople 22, 26, 31, 32, 35, 36, 90, 94
Cordoba in Spain 50
Coroni??) in Ac(h)a(i)ea 52
Cous (island) 40
Cratia (in Bithynia) 39
Cy(i)clades islands 20

Dacia/Dacia Ripensis 36, 51, 52
Dalmatia 20
Dardania 51
Dioclec(t)ianopolis in Mac(h)edonia 31, 50
Dium in Mac(h)edonia 52
Docimium (in Phrygia) 38
Doliche (in Syria) 38
Dori(y)lai(e)um (in Phrygia) 39

Egypt 44, 52, 64, 71
Elatea in Ac(h)a(i)ea 51

Elida in Ac(h)a(i)ea 31, 51
Emerita 50

Emimontus = H(a)emimontus [= Balkan mountains] 20
Eph(f)esus in Asia 38, 46, 50
Epiphania (in Syria) 39
Eraclia Linci in Mac(h)edonia 51
Europe 20

Filadelfia (in Lydia) 39
Filippi in Mac(h)edonia 50
Filippopolis (in Thrace) [= Plovdiv] 41
Foenicia 20
F(ph)r(i)ygia 20

Gabula (in Syria) 41
Galat(c)ia 20, 21, 26, 46
Gaul 35, 28, 52, 95
Gannos in Thrace 50
Gaza in Palestine 26, 38, 46, 50
Germanicia (in Syria) 39

Hellespontus 20
Heraclia (in Europe) 38, 45
(H)Ieropolis (in Phrygia) 40

Ilium 40
Illyricum 98
Irenopolis (in Cilicia) = Neronias 40, 50
Isauria 20
Iscus in Dacia Ripensis 52
Italy 28, 50, 51, 74, 96, 98

Juliopolis (in Galatia) 39

Larissa (in Thessaly) 51
Laudo(i)cia (= Laodicea) (in Phrygia) 40, 45, 50
Letus (in Egypt) 40

Licia (in Pisidia) 40
Li(y)dia 20
Lignidus/Lychnidus (in the Epirus) 51

Li(y)sinia (in Pisidia) 38
Luca in Tuscia 50
Lyons/Lugdunum in Gaul 52

Macaria in Ac(h)ai(e)a 51
Mac(h)edonia 25, 50, 51, 52
Magnesia (in Asia) 39
Mareota(is) (in Egypt)30, 39, 45, 52
Megara in Ac(h)ai(e)a 51
Mesopotamia 20
Milan/Mediolanum 51, 54, 56, 69, 73, 84
Miletus (in Asia) 40
Mo(a)esia 46
Mopsu(e)s(tia) in Cilicia 36, 38
Motoni in Ac(h)ai(e)a 52
Mui(y)rsa in Pannonia [= Osijek] 46, 50

Naisus (in Dacia) 51
Naupactus in Ac(h)ai(e)a 51
Neapolis (= Naples) in Campania 20, 51
Neocaesarea (in Pontus) 40
Neronias (= Irenopolis) 45
Nicea in Bithynia 60, 61, 64, 74, 83, 84, 95, 97, 98
Nic(h)e(a) (in Thrace) 86, 92, 93
Nicomedia (in Bithynia) 20
Nicopolis (in Epirus) 51

Palestine 20, 25, 26, 46, 50, 51
Pamphi(y)lia 20
Pannonia the Pannonias 25, 46, 51
Paf(ph)lagonia 20
Paris 93
Parnasus (in Cappadocia) 39
Particopolis in Mac(h)edonia 51

Patras in Ac(h)a(i)a 51
Pelusium in Egypt 40, 103
Pergamum (in Asia) 39
Pergamum (in Thrace) 40

Perge (in Pamphylia) 40
Philadelphia, Philetus, Philippi   see Fil-
Phoenicia, see Foenicia
Phrygia, see Frigia
Pisidia 20
Polidiane (in Phoenicia) 39
Pontus 20

Raphania (in Syria) 38
Ravenna 51
Rimini (Ariminum) 20, 71, 80, 82, 83, 86, 87, 88, 90, 93, 94, 95, 100
Rome 27, 28, 35, 36, 42, 47, 48, 70, 71, 72, 79
Rosus (in Cilicia) 38

Salona in Dalmatia 20
Samosata 21
Sa(e)rdica [= modern Sophia] 20, 28, 29, 33, 41, 42, 46, 51, 56, 57,
         59, 64, 65, 71
Sardinia 50
Savia (province) 52
Scirus in Ac(h)ai(e)a 51
Scupi in Dardania 51
Seleucia [= modern Silifke] 90
Sicily 50
Singidunum in Moesia [= modern Belgrade] 46, 50, 100
Sinopa in Helenopontus 39
Si(y)rmium [= modern Sremska Mitrovica] 54, 56, 78
Siscia in Savia 52
Spain 50
Spoleto/Spoletium 76
Syria 20, 32

Tenedos in Asia 51

Terasia (in the Cyclades) 51
T(h)essalonica in Mac(h)edonia 32, 51
Thanis (in Egypt) 40
Thebes (H)eptapilos in Ac(h)a(i)ea 51
Thebes in T(h)essaly 50

Thebais(d) 20
Thenus (in the Cyclades) 40
T(h)essaly 51
Thrace/ r(h)rac(h)ia 20, 50, 51, 86, 92
Triveri [= Trier] 19, 36
Troas (in the Hellespont) 40
Trocnada (in Galatia) 39
Tuscia [= Etruria] 50
Tyre (in Phoenicia) 25, 39

Ulpiani in Dardania 51
Ustodizo see Nic(h)e(a)

Verona 51

(H)Ypata in T(h)essaly 51

Zela in (Helenopontus) 39
Zeuma (in Syria) 38

TRANSLATED TEXTS FOR HISTORIANS
Published Titles

Gregory of Tours: Life of the Fathers
Translated with an introduction by EDWARD JAMES
Volume 1: 176pp., 2nd edition 1991, ISBN 0 85323 327 6

The Emperor Julian: Panegyric and Polemic
Claudius Mamertinus, John Chrysostom, Ephrem the Syrian
edited by SAMUEL N. C. LIEU
Volume 2: 153pp., 2nd edition 1989, ISBN 0 85323 376 4

Pacatus: Panegyric to the Emperor Theodosius
Translated with an introduction by C. E. V. NIXON
Volume 3: 122pp., 1987, ISBN 0 85323 076 5

Gregory of Tours: Glory of the Martyrs
Translated with an introduction by RAYMOND VAN DAM
Volume 4: 150pp., 1988, ISBN 0 85323 236 9

Gregory of Tours: Glory of the Confessors
Translated with an introduction by RAYMOND VAN DAM
Volume 5: 127pp., 1988, ISBN 0 85323 226 1

The Book of Pontiffs (*Liber Pontificalis* to AD 715)
Translated with an introduction by RAYMOND DAVIS
Volume 6: 175pp., 1989, ISBN 0 85323 216 4

Chronicon Paschale 284–628 AD
Translated with notes and introduction by
MICHAEL WHITBY AND MARY WHITBY
Volume 7: 280pp., 1989, ISBN 0 85323 096 X

Iamblichus: On the Pythagorean Life
Translated with notes and introduction by GILLIAN CLARK
Volume 8: 144pp., 1989, ISBN 0 85323 326 8

Conquerors and Chroniclers of Early-Medieval Spain
Translated with notes and introduction by KENNETH BAXTER WOLF
Volume 9: 176pp., 1991, ISBN 0 85323 047 1

Victor of Vita: History of the Vandal Persecution
Translated with notes and introduction by JOHN MOORHEAD
Volume 10: 112pp., 1992, ISBN 0 85323 426 4

The Goths in the Fourth Century
by PETER HEATHER AND JOHN MATTHEWS
Volume 11: 224pp., 1992, ISBN 0 85323 426 4

Cassiodorus: *Variae*
Translated with notes and introduction by S. J. B. BARNISH
Volume 12: 260pp., 1992, ISBN 0 85323 436 1

The Lives of the Eighth-Century Popes (*Liber Pontificalis*)
Translated with an introduction and commentary by RAYMOND DAVIS
Volume 13: 288pp., 1992, ISBN 0 85323 018 8

Eutropius: Breviarium
Translated with an introduction and commentary by H. W. BIRD
Volume 14: 248pp., 1993, ISBN 0 85323 208 3

The Seventh Century in the West-Syrian Chronicles
Introduced, translated and annotated by ANDREW PALMER
including two Seventh-century Syriac apocalyptic texts
Introduced, translated and annotated by SEBASTIAN BROCK
with added annotation and an historical introduction by ROBERT HOYLAND
Volume 15: 368pp., 1993, ISBN 0 85323 238 5

Vegetius: Epitome of Military Science
Translated with notes and introduction by N. P. MILNER
Volume 16: 208pp., 2nd edition 1996, ISBN 0 85323 910 X

Aurelius Victor: De Caesaribus
Translated with an introduction and commentary by H. W. BIRD
Volume 17: 264pp., 1994, ISBN 0-85323-218-0

Bede: On the Tabernacle
Translated with notes and introduction by ARTHUR G. HOLDER
Volume 18: 224pp., 1994, ISBN 0-85323-378-0

Caesarius of Arles: Life, Testament, Letters
Translated with notes and introduction by William E. Klingshirn
Volume 19: 176pp. 1994, ISBN 085323 368-3

The Lives of the Ninth-Century Popes (*Liber Pontificalis*)
Translated with an introduction and commentary by RAYMOND DAVIS
Volume 20: 360pp., 1995, ISBN 0-85323-479-5

Bede: On the Temple
Translated with notes by SEÁN CONNOLLY,
introduction by JENNIFER O'REILLY
Volume 21: 192pp., 1995, ISBN 0-85323-049-8

Pseudo-Dionysius of Tel-Mahre: *Chronicle*, **Part III**
Translated with notes and introduction by WITOLD WITAKOWSKI
Volume 22: 192pp., 1995, ISBN 0-85323-760-3

Venantius Fortunatus: Personal and Political Poems
Translated with notes and introduction by JUDITH GEORGE
Volume 23: 192pp., 1995, ISBN 0-85323-179-6

Donatist Martyr Stories: The Church in Conflict in Roman North Africa
Translated with notes and introduction by MAUREEN A. TILLEY
Volume 24: 144pp., 1996, ISBN 0 85323 931 2

Hilary of Poitiers: Conflicts of Conscience and Law in the Fourth-Century Church
Translated with Introduction and notes by LIONEL R. WICKHAM
Volume 25, 133pp., 1997, ISBN 085323-572-4

Lives of the Visigothic Fathers
Translated and edited by A. T. Fear
Volume 26: 208pp., 1997, ISBN 0-85323-582-1

Optatus: Against the Donatists
Translated with Notes and Introduction by MARK J. EDWARDS
Volume 27: 220pp., 1997, ISBN 085323-752-2

For full details of Translated Texts for Historians, including prices and ordering information, please write to the following:

All countries, except the USA and Canada: Liverpool University Press, Senate House, Abercromby Square, Liverpool, L69 3BX, UK (*Tel* 0151-794 2233, *Fax* 0151-794 2235).
USA and Canada: University of Pennsylvania Press, 4200 Pine Street, Philadelphia, PA 19104–4011, USA (*Tel* (215) 898-6264, *Fax* (215) 898-0404).